# Consumer Behaviour and Social Network Sites

This book provides a solid understanding of electronic word of mouth (eWOM) by taking the reader through the process of information diffusion from rumour generation in times of traditional word of mouth (WOM) to negative social eWOM and examining how consumers process it.

*Consumer Behaviour and Social Network Sites* tackles different themes relating to negative eWOM. Drawing on both intensive scientific research and professional examples, it bridges the gap between the academic and professional worlds. The book contrasts negative social eWOM to traditional WOM while discussing the specificities of different social networking sites in diffusing such information. It looks at why and how consumers decide to create, share and react to negative social eWOM, suggesting that there are more reasons than are commonly presumed for consumers to articulate themselves on these platforms. It also provides an appreciation of web users' behaviours with regards to negative social eWOM and how it can alter their decision-making journey.

The book concludes with several strategies and key takeaways to deal with and prevent negative social eWOM. Most books on WOM are purely professional and lack the theoretical contextualization of the issue. Moreover, they often provide insights on brand-to-consumer conversation but not consumer-to-consumer (C2C) communication. This short book provides marketing academics, students and practitioners with an important insight into these C2C communications that can potentially be harmful to brands.

**Sarah Zaraket** received her PhD in Management Sciences at Pantheon-Sorbonne University, Paris, France. She conducts research on consumer behaviour on social media and has taught several courses on digital marketing, research methodology and innovation. Sarah has assisted many brands in successfully building their social media strategies.

# Routledge Focus on Business and Management

The fields of business and management have grown exponentially as areas of research and education. This growth presents challenges for readers trying to keep up with the latest important insights. Routledge Focus on Business and Management presents small books on big topics and how they intersect with the world of business research.

Individually, each title in the series provides coverage of a key academic topic, whilst collectively the series forms a comprehensive collection across the business disciplines.

**Entrepreneurial Urban Regeneration**
Business Improvement Districts as a Form of Organizational Innovation
*Rezart Prifti and Fatma Jaupi*

**Strategic University Management**
Future Proofing Your Institution
*Loren Falkenberg and M. Elizabeth Cannon*

**Innovation in Africa**
Fuelling an Entrepreneurial Ecosystem for Growth and Prosperity
*Deseye Umurhohwo*

**Consumer Behaviour and Social Network Sites**
The Impact of Negative Word of Mouth
*Sarah Zaraket*

**Artificial Intelligence in Accounting**
Practical Applications
*Cory Ng and John Alarcon*

For more information about this series, please visit: www.routledge.com/ Routledge-Focus-on-Business-and-Management/book-series/FBM

# Consumer Behaviour and Social Network Sites
## The Impact of Negative Word of Mouth

**Sarah Zaraket**

Routledge
Taylor & Francis Group

LONDON AND NEW YORK

First published 2021
by Routledge
2 Park Square, Milton Park, Abingdon, Oxon OX14 4RN

and by Routledge
52 Vanderbilt Avenue, New York, NY 10017

*Routledge is an imprint of the Taylor & Francis Group, an informa business*

© 2021 Sarah Zaraket

The right of Sarah Zaraket to be identified as author of this work
has been asserted by her in accordance with sections 77 and 78 of the
Copyright, Designs and Patents Act 1988.

*British Library Cataloguing-in-Publication Data*
A catalogue record for this book is available from the British Library

*Library of Congress Cataloging-in-Publication Data*
A catalog record has been requested for this book

ISBN: 978-0-367-53283-3 (hbk)
ISBN: 978-1-003-08127-2 (ebk)

Typeset in Times New Roman
by Newgen Publishing UK

To my father. The first person that liked and shared my story long before Facebook ever existed. Thank you for always being a beacon of positivity and truth even when it was easier to spread negative words ...

# Contents

# Figures

# Acknowledgements

I've always been fascinated by words and how people use them to tell their stories. The story of the influence of words is one I've wanted to tell for a while now. I would like to thank every single person that contributed in making this story see the light of day. Thank you to the outstanding people at Routledge for their follow up and their undeniable professionalism, even during tough times. Thank you to my amazingly supportive friends. Thank you to my incredible brothers, the light of my life. Thank you to my one of a kind father who instilled in me the love of knowledge and intellectual curiosity. Thank you to my guardian angel and eternal source of inspiration, my mother, not a day goes by where I don't miss you more.

# Introduction

*You're in a restaurant, the food arrives and it's not cooked through. You complain to the waiter who tells you he can't do anything about it. You then decide to take it up with the manager. But you can't get a hold of him. You feel disgusted and ripped off. So what do you do? Typically, you have two choices, either you let it go and do nothing or you take action. Ten years ago, you might have opted for the first option. But not today, today, you're more likely to take action.*

In this day and age consumers feel so empowered they will not tolerate bad service delivery. All they have to do is take a picture and post it on social media. It's that easy to exercise pressure on the company. In fact, many of them never fail to mention it, threatening brands with their reputations. Every person is equipped with a smartphone and can take pictures anywhere, anytime, which can potentially cause a threat. Today's consumer is always on his smartphone consuming and sharing content. Evidently, smartphones have become an extension of one's hand. It's no wonder it's becoming a reflex to document brand failures and share them online so they can reach a maximum number of people, starting with one's network. Social media have made this task so easy it's become second nature to users. In addition, consumers are increasingly following a ROBO pattern (read online buy offline) or web influenced in store sales (Vanheems, 2018). In fact, 94 percent of consumers claim an online review has convinced them to avoid a business (ReviewTrackers, 2018). This omni canalization has made it important to analyze online platforms, which are the source of consumer behavior, in order to predict and react to consumer actions.

This electronic word of mouth on social media is now one of the most influential communication channels and its appeal to businesses is well established (Zhang et al., 2017). As a result, professionals and academics have grasped the importance of this new and increasingly popular form of communication. However, academic work has mainly focused on the positive side of social media, such as the benefits of building strong relationships between the brand and consumers and sharing positive word of mouth. And yet, few researchers tackled the dark side of social media. It's more likely that you will find books about inciting positive word of mouth than ones tackling negative word of mouth. This is regretful, since negative word of mouth has never been more relevant than today. There's a growing need to understand why consumers create and share these messages on social media they way they do. The world post Covid-19 is a world of drastic change. Many movements have taken the world by storm as consumers are increasingly demanding more ethical consumption choices and actively marking their disapproval of any kind of company wrongdoing. There is no more room for messing up. Consequently, many brands have shifted their marketing and communication strategies accordingly.

The fact of the matter remains that marketers see this form of communication lies beyond their immediate control: it is customer centric—not firm-centric—yet they would like to have a better understanding of it and be more responsive to it (East & Uncles, 2008). This book will remedy this issue, it will give insights on what makes consumers *TIK* when exposed to a negative situation and what makes them *TOK* negatively about brands on social network sites.

# 1 Once upon a word…

Where did speech come from? Long before the written word, humans communicated through different means. From the drawings on the Chauvet caves to mimicry and movements, to the Greeks' rhetoric art, mankind has always strived to connect. Before delving into the written word, an overview of the evolution of speech is essential.

At one point in time, the mere thought of theorizing about the birth of speech was heavily frowned upon. In fact, in the 1860s, the British Academy, as well as the Société Linguistique de Paris, discouraged their members from speculating about those origins. It was believed that these debates would only lead to pointless assumptions (Hockett & Hockett, 1960). A century later, deliberations were once again possible. The time was finally right to lead these investigations as new ways of thinking and new techniques emerged. Over the last decades, studies on the matter exploded.

Nevertheless, the lines remain blurred concerning the beginning of speech. It was clear that no consensus would be reached soon. However, what was certain is the fact that fully developed language was present 50 000 years ago in Europe where humans created art and buried the dead, a sign of the existence of fluent language (Holden, 2004). Speech evolved with the physiological development of human speech organs that are used in language such as vocal organs, the lips, and the tongue. It is believed that the ancient mother tongue spoken by first modern humans is the *click language*, which relies on adept tongue and inward air movement (Holden, 2004).

Once speech was born, it was only a matter of time before it was put together to create a story. People love stories and have been telling them for a long time. From drawing tales of hunting adventures on caves in the prehistoric era to narrating the Mesopotamian Epic of Gilgamesh and the Ancient Greek Odyssey, sharing stories has always been a tool to entertain, educate, preserve culture or even preach moral values.

These oral traditions of storytelling can be thought of as the first form of word of mouth. Before the invention of writing and the printing press, engaging in word of mouth was the easiest way to communicate. This idiom has been used since the 1500s; it is the anglicization of the Latin idiom *viva voce*, which translates to living voice (Word of mouth Idiom Definition – Grammarist, 2020). Word of mouth entails the oral exchange of information between individuals, it has shaped the way we pass on tradition, and relay the history of the world, as well as communicate on common interests.

## Rumors or word of mouth?

People often relate word of mouth to rumors. Early work on rumors, dating back several centuries, had already emphasized its negative and unstable character. Several fields have then seized this notion to study the mechanisms of influence of information conveyed by word of mouth.

Rumor is derived from the Latin word *rumor* that means confusing noise that runs. Rumors ran for centuries before being considered an object of scientific research. The first known attempt at a definition dates back to the seventeenth century where the first definitions focused on their slanderous and irrational aspect (Brodin & Roux, 1990). Louis William Stern (1902) defines the rumor as "*a chain of subjects who tell each other a story of word-of-mouth, without repetition or explanation; at the end, we compare the story told by the first subject and the story told by the last; naturally, history is at best truncated, at worst distorted.*" Thus, the German sociologist was the first to refer to the uncertain aspect of the rumor and the change that it undergoes over time. As of the second half of the twentieth century, research on rumors increased in a cyclical logic. The rumors spoke of major events that marked public opinions such as wars or pandemics. During the Second World War, when rumors became a full-fledged war strategy, early definitions of word of mouth appeared with the work of Allport and Postman (1946). In the footsteps of L. W. Sterne, the two psychologists have revealed three characteristics of word of mouth similar to rumors: leveling, sharpening, and assimilation. *Leveling* suggests that the message gets shorter with fewer details as it gets diffused in later versions. *Sharpening* refers to the fact that the predominant information remains in the storyline and is not removed in future versions; it includes selective retention of information. Finally, *assimilation* is the "noise" people add as they retell the rumor through their own linguistic specificities and cognitive biases. It can be linked to distortion since it refers to the integration of one's attitude, beliefs, and subconscious. According to Breck and Cardie's (2004) broken phone syndrome, positive information gets shorter and is not distorted while negative information gets longer in later versions and is distorted. The definitions of rumor have increased since then, but they all agree on the characteristics mentioned earlier, namely, the arbitrary aspect of the speech, the changing content as it is transmitted, and the validity of the story, almost impossible to verify.

More recently, Roquette (1979) has developed four characteristics of the rumor: the implication of the transmitter, the impossibility of verifying the transmitted content, the negativity, and the distortion of the message. A few years later, the notion of rumor marketing is introduced in France (Kapferer, 1990). The author is one of the pioneers to have considered word of mouth as mass media. He develops a definition that will then serve as a theoretical basis for research on rumors, particularly in the field of marketing communication and brand awareness. According to the author, a rumor is "*the emergence and circulation of social information that is neither confirmed nor denied publicly by official sources.*" Inscribing the rumor in an individual frame, but also in the social frame, we can draw a list of motivations that push an individual to relay this type of information. According to the author, individuals need to speak-to-speak, speak-to-know, speak-to-please, and finally speak-to-convince.

Rumor is then conveyed through word-of-mouth, which is defined as an interpersonal oral transmission between a transmitter and a receiver where the communicant is perceived as non-commercial (Arendt, 1967). Several areas are quickly taking hold of this nascent concept of word of mouth. We can mention, to name a few: social communication, social psychology, information sciences, and later, management sciences. The focus of this book is the latter.

## Towards a comprehensive definition of WOM

As research regarding WOM evolved, many different definitions have emerged, such as Westbrook's (1987) definition in which he specifies the subject matter of the communication and incorporates the services factor that was lacking in Arendt's definition. Buttle (1998) also adds an important contribution when he explains that the information can be positive or negative. Additionally, Stokes et al. (2002) stipulate that WOM is an interpersonal communication about products or services in which the sender perceives the receiver to be impartial. This mention

*Table 1.1* WOM definition

| Informal Communication | The term informal refers to an unorganized behavior. Word of mouth consists on sharing information, thoughts or ideas. It can be either positive or negative (Buttle, 1998). |
| A sender and a receiver | WOM occurs between friends and family, it almost does not happen anonymously. |
| No commercial aim | It is considered to be more effective than advertising because it is perceived to be unbiased (Stokes et al., 2002) |

of impartiality relates to the receivers' perception towards the source. Stokes et al. (2002) were the first to introduce the notion of how individuals perceive the source and their belief in them. Similarly, Litvin et al. (2008) highlight a defining characteristic of WOM: the independence of the source. Some authors speak of consumer-to-consumer communication (Gruen et al., 2006).

Based on the previous definitions we can, therefore, retain a broad definition of classical word of mouth as a consumer-to-consumer informal exchange of positive or negative information about a product or a service serving no commercial intent. A review of the WOM definition is presented in Table 1.1.

## WOM in marketing: the birth of WOMM

The power and potential of word of mouth have pushed marketers to integrate this phenomenon in their marketing strategies. The first person to recognize the benefits of this informal communication was psychologist George Silverman. In 1970, he conducted a study where physicians were asked to discuss new pharmaceutical products. He soon realized that even the most skeptical of doctors were influenced by the positive feedbacks of their peers. It was so powerful that even physicians who had previously endured a negative experience with the products changed their minds following their peers' positive reviews (Pandey et al., 2017). Silverman was the pioneer of word of mouth marketing (WOMM).

Word of mouth marketing is the intentional influencing of consumer-to-consumer communications through marketing techniques (Kozinets et al., 2010). This phenomenon was so powerful that the Word of Mouth Marketing Association (WOMMA) was created in 2004 to ethically lead and advocate for the WOM industry through education, professional development, networking, and knowledge sharing. It was acquired in 2018 by ANA (Association of National Advertisers) (Wolfe, 2018). Word of mouth marketing drives $6 trillion of annual consumer spending and is believed to constitute 13 percent of consumer sales. Moreover, WOMM impression yields five times more sales than paid media impression (Saleh, n.d.). In fact, people are more likely to believe their friends than other marketing sources since peer influence is 5000 times more effective than traditional marketing (Silverman, 2009).

Over the years, professional as well as academic studies on WOMM have exploded. Professional books on how to generate and use WOMM have piqued the interest of businesses (Kelly, 2007; Rosen, 2009; Sernovitz et al., 2006) while researchers continued to explore the antecedents and consequences of this phenomenon (Kozinets et al., 2010; Cheung et al., 2009).

The power of WOM resides in the fact that consumers prefer to get information from their peers, which makes WOM the most trusted source of information since it's independent, impartial, and informal (Derbaix & Vanhamme, 2003). In parallel, WOM has become a more effective marketing tool (Goldsmith & Horowitz, 2006). In fact, WOM has an impact on consumer behavior and can influence their preferences (Godes & Mayzlin, 2004).

Furthermore, research has shown that WOM influences product decisions, selecting service providers (Price & Feick, 1984; Lau & Ng, 2001; Keaveney, 1995) and reducing risk and uncertainty of choice (Olshavsky & Granbois, 1979). Consumers make an effort while deciding on their next purchase. Other consumers' recommendations reduce these efforts and the uncertainty of making a decision by making it easier to decide on a purchase (Fitzsimons & Lehman, 2004).

## Identifying persuasion mechanisms to better understand WOM

Persuasive communication has been the subject of much research in various fields: psychology, sociology, social communication, etc. Research in the field of medical persuasion has uncovered more than 15 theories belonging to different categories: theories of attitude, cognitive theories, functional approaches, cognitive biases, and others (Cameron, 2009). Historically, the scientific community recognizes two distinct origins of work on persuasion. The first essays, of artistic origin, are attributed to Aristotle and go back to more than three centuries BC where the latter had already defined, by means of the treatise of the rhetoric, the arguments of the persuasion and the effects that it is necessary to arouse in the receiver to convince him (De Barnier, 2006). He was the first to lay the groundwork for social influence and persuasion (BERSCHEID, 1976). During the Second World War a second approach of the attitude was born, a more scientific one. Carl Hovland's experimental empirical research has been a major turning point in this area. Unlike his predecessor's work that focuses on the receiver, Hovland was more interested in the source and form of the message. Three currents then emerged: work based on the contribution of Hovland, which focused on the sender; those who study the form and structure of the message (Hovland et al., 1953; McGuire, 1969); and finally, those who are interested in the receiver (Petty & Cacioppo, 1981). This trilogy dominated the field of persuasive research until the emergence of foundational works on advertising persuasion adopting a more holistic approach. The ELM (Elaboration Likelihood Model) model that Petty and Cacioppo developed in 1981 embodied this holistic approach. This gave rise to many works that attempted to study persuasion and its underlying mechanisms, cognitive but also emotional. Researchers then approached more interactive and complementary approaches (Holbrook & Hirschman, 1982; Zajonc, 1980), giving birth to a new era: that of persuasion through the double process of persuasion, also called the persuasion routes. Therefore, it is no longer a question of a single persuasion process but of a multitude of mechanisms acting alone, together or intertwined (Chaiken & Eagly, 1983; Greenwald & Leavitt, 1984; Mitchell, 1981, Petty & Cacioppo, 1981). It goes without saying that this trend has created a strong divergence among the scientific community as to the number of routes involved and their modes of interaction. Overall, the theory of persuasion was based on a simple questioning: how can we persuade individuals to change their attitude. Is it with the right arguments?

Persuasive communication is based on the traditional theory of communication and is comprised of the same elements. Going back to the theory of classical communication, Lasswell (1948) proposed the following formula: "Who says what to whom, in what channel with what effect." In other words, communication consists of five components: the transmitter ("who"), the message ("what"), the receiver ("who"), the support ("channel with what effect"). Figure 1.1 illustrates the basic communication model. Each one of these components of word of mouth communication will be mentioned at the end of this chapter. It's important at this stage to focus on the interest of this book: negative WOM.

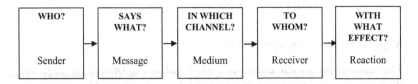

*Figure 1.1* The classical model of communication

# Negative WOM

## What is negative WOM?

Negative WOM is defined as the derogatory information transmitted from a sender to a receiver with the objective of denigrating a product, emphasizing a compliant or an unsatisfying experience (Hornik et al., 2015). It entails talking about a failure. This failure can take one of two forms: performance-based failure and value-based failure. A performance-based failure refers to a product's or a service's failure whereas a value-based failure refers to a company's ethical and social transgressions.

Performance-based failures can be related to defective products such as Toyota's brakes (Liker, 2011), product shortage (Copulsky, 2011), or other product-related deficiencies. It also includes service failures such as dragging a passenger out of an overbooked flight (Victor & Stevens, 2017), late shipments, interaction failures (excessive wait line, bad customer care, and so on), and other service-related insufficiencies. Negative WOM generated about these shortcomings is usually conducted by consumers (vs. non-consumers) who have experienced them first hand.

Value-based failures are not related to the product or service itself but to the brand's values. They manifest through the brand's public behavior. Sometimes, these values are transmitted through the company's philosophy and brand identity while other times they take the shape of an unsocial or unethical behavior (such as child labor, animal testing, and so on). Among these value-based failures, Hansen et al., (2018) distinguish between social failure and communication failures. The latter include offensive messages or a miscommunication displayed by the brand (e.g., Bud Light Beer's slogan: The perfect beer for removing 'no' from your vocabulary for the night, Strom, 2015) whereas the former represents a breach of social values such as Amazon's poor working conditions (Guendelsberger, 2019).

## Negative WOM vs positive WOM

The debate on which communication valence (positive vs negative WOM) is more influential has not yet been resolved. On one hand, positive WOM seems to win the upper hand as it is said to affect purchase intention more than negative WOM (East et al., 2008). Moreover, positive WOM attracts new consumers who are likely to perceive the product as desirable based on WOM (Wu & Wang, 2011). If a consumer is already tempted to purchase a brand, positive eWOM can increase his chances of making that purchase over buying another brand (East et al., 2008). Other authors argue that negative word of mouth is more influential than positive word of mouth and is transmitted to more people as it gains more attention.

Nevertheless, there seems to be a consensus between marketing practitioners and academics that negative WOM (NWOM) is more influential than positive WOM (East et al., 2008). Many studies showed that people tend to believe negative WOM more than positive WOM (Huang et al., 2011; Lau & Ng, 2001), this leads to the *negativity bias* (Hornik et al., 2015). One reason could be that commercials are generally positive, so when a negative message arises, it offsets the positive environment, therefore receiving more attention (Chakravarty et al., 2010). Arndt (1967) found that negative WOM had twice as much influence on the recipient than positive WOM. However, he was criticized for reviewing only one brand whereas systematic research has to be conducted over brands and categories to draw valid affirmations (East et al., 2008). Dubois et al. (2016) argue that people tend to share more negative WOM with their close peers and more positive WOM with others to protect their close friends and family and assert self-enhancement to others. Besides its influence on its recipients, what makes NWOM dangerous for brands?

## Some impacts of negative WOM

As we've previously seen, rumor dissemination can occur very quickly, the social impact theory stipulates that people transfer information to other individuals, which creates rumor diffusion. Since people tend to believe negative WOM more than positive WOM because this information travels faster and reaches a larger number of individuals than other kinds of information (Hornik et al., 2015).

Furthermore, the impact that negative word of mouth has on companies is considerable. A negative eWOM posted by one consumer can reach thousands of potential consumers at a simple click of a button. Research has shown that a consumer's willingness to engage in negative eWOM can have an impact on a firm's reputation (Holloway & Beatty, 2003). In fact, when a potential consumer views the negative feedback, he might get distrust and a negative attitude towards the brand (Wang, 2010). Also, negative eWOM has a higher effect on consumer purchase decisions than positive eWOM (Chang & Wu, 2014). In fact, the impact of negative on decreasing sales is bigger than positive on increasing it (Park & Lee, 2009).

Before discussing negative WOM components, it's important to raise the following question: how has technology changed negative WOM?

## From clicks back to clicks... How the Internet gave rise to electronic word of mouth (eWOM)

As mentioned at the beginning of this chapter, one of the first forms of communication was clicks. Technology has brought word of mouth back to its ancestor route. From click language to using online clicks as a means of communication, the Internet has completely transformed the way in which communication takes place. This will revolutionize consumer habits by taking on new challenges for consumers. Special interest is given to this phenomenon by researchers and practitioners. Studies of the characteristics of electronic word of mouth (eWOM) and its influence mechanisms have concluded that the web and digital media have transformed this new form of communication from traditional interpersonal communication. New entities will then take part in this communication and a more holistic innovative vision is born. All of these will be discussed in detail in what follows.

### *From word of mouth (WOM) to electronic word of mouth (eWOM)*

Traditional word of mouth was limited to the immediate social sphere and its influence was characterized by the very limited scope and rapid decrease in space and time (Gauri et al., 2008). However, with the advent of the Internet, research on WOM has been extended to its electronic form (Cheung et al., 2009). In an electronic word of mouth communication the information is relayed quickly and indefinitely by other users to other platforms (Phelps et al., 2004). Thus, messages broadcast to friends or family for the attention of a very small number of individuals are now likely to be within reach of the world within a few clicks. Today, making a buzz or going viral is one of the most recognized forms of this effect in terms of impact on brands. Thus, digital media has given WOM attributes that have radically transformed it: an instantaneous propagation speed and global reach (Phelps et al., 2004). This is what makes eWOM one of the major concerns of companies.

The characteristics of WOM cited earlier, namely the distortions of the message and the loss of the original source of the information will be amplified in the digital context (Towner & Dulio, 2011). Whereas part of what we know about WOM likely applies to eWOM, other factors are likely impacted by the characteristics of this digital form.

As research in eWOM is increasing, so are its comprehensive definitions. One of the most quoted definitions in the literature remains that of Hennig-Thurau et al. (2004). According to the authors, eWOM represents

> any form of positive or negative declaration made by old, poten-
> tial or actual customers on a product or service of a company and
> which is made available over the Internet by a multitude of people
> as well as the company. It can be exchanged through a variety of
> media such as e-mail, instant messaging, home pages, blogs, forums,
> virtual communities, consumer protection sites, critical sites, and
> evaluation of products as well as social networking sites.

It recollects all the WOM elements and specifies that it is online. Even though this definition is popular in the marketing literature, it received some criticism. In fact, Xun and Reynolds (2010) believe that the definition limits eWOM to a still conceptualization and does not value the dynamic information exchange. Web users rely on eWOM to make more informed decisions and to reduce the risks associated with the absence of direct contact when purchasing online (Awad, 2008).

## Word of Mouth (WOM) and Electronic Word of Mouth (eWOM): similar yet divergent

Electronic word of mouth shares a number of features with traditional word of mouth. The most evident resemblance between WOM and eWOM concern some aspects of their definition and their characteristics. Both WOM and eWOM represent interpersonal communication between consumers and bidirectional and interactive communication. In terms of consequences, they both influence attitude and purchasing behaviors (Cheung & Thadani, 2012; Hu et al., 2008). However, they remain different in many respects (Cheung & Thadani, 2012). These new characteristics induced by digital technologies make eWOM a particular form of communication that deserves to be looked at closer.

*The scope of the message*

The first point concerns the scope of the message. In the past, WOM was a form of face-to-face interpersonal communication while eWOM is evolving on Internet platforms. The information contained in the message was then shared among groups of limited individuals and synchronously during private conversations (Avery et al., 1999; Dellarocas et al., 2007; Steffes and Burgee, 2009). It is thus difficult to transmit the content to people who are not physically present at the time of sharing. Individuals may in turn relay this content in their private sphere, but the scope of the message in question remains relatively limited. It will at best be broadcast in the immediate environment of the subject. On the other hand, electronic communication takes place across multiple paths and asynchronously (Hung & Li, 2007). The different receivers are not required to be present at the moment and at the very place where the bearer of the message proceeds to broadcast it (Karakaya & Barnes, 2010), which calls into question the interpersonal character of this communication. For example, consumers can post information about their experiences of consuming products and services. The media that serve as a place for exchange can take many forms: communities dedicated to online reviews such as TripAdvisor or Yelp, thematic blogs, and blogs of expert users, discussion forums, etc. Once a discussion is created or a review is published, any individual can read or interact with the content of the topic at once or later. The information remains available on the web for an indefinite period. Due to its low cost and high speed of propagation, eWOM is then considered as a form of communication exponentially more influential and more effective than the traditional form (Hamouda & Tabbane, 2014).

*Sustainability and accessibility*

The second characteristic of eWOM derives from the previous one and relates to the durable and accessible nature of its content. The user-generated information is available to the receivers for an unlimited period of time (Hennig-Thurau et al., 2004; Breazeale, 2009). In addition, it should be noted that, in some areas characterized by obsolescence and renewal, the relevance of information may be obsolete if it is consulted after a certain period of time (McKinney et al., 2002).

A study on the news of online reviews, conducted by Jin et al. (2014) highlighted the importance of the temporal variable. The latter limits the validity and therefore the impact of electronic word-of-mouth through the psychological distance created between information and consumers.

## The available and observable nature of the eWOM

The third difference also follows the second. The availability and observability of this new form of communication offer researchers an unprecedented opportunity in terms of analysis and study. Henderson and Gilding (2004), as well as Sun et al. (2006), point out that eWOM is characterized by its measurability, unlike traditional WOM. In addition, the ease of estimating message content provides receivers with measurable, richer, and more structured information with respect to traditional WOM (Chatterjee, 2001). These attributes result in an estimate of the number of messages, their presentation form, and the persistence of their content over time. In this regard, Qiu et al. (2012) point to another benefit for customers seeking information online. It is about the fact that consumers can cross a lot of information and be able to instantly compare the different points of view, something inconceivable with traditional WOM, which is less available, less tangible, and more ephemeral.

## The anonymity of the source

Cheung and Thadani (2012) highlight a crucial point that distinguishes eWOM from its predecessor and concerns the impersonal aspect of this type of communication. This is the source of the message and the link that the receiver has with the author. When the sender of the message is known and identified, the content is often poor and of limited scope, at least in terms of the digital content available today. In addition, the rich and durable information that we can consult today at any time on the web often emanates from a transmitter, which is completely unknown to us. This factor will give the researchers a hard time later. The source was once known to the receiver and credibility was thus fully established, unlike online communication where the web user in search of information often knows very little about the source. Therefore, reliability and expertise are questionable. Thus, the credibility of eWOM and that of the source emitting is at the heart of the vast majority of studies on the impact of eWOM (Cheung & Thadani, 2012).

## Different types of eWOM

To define the eWOM in a more developed way it is necessary at first to identify the different types of eWOM before presenting its components. Xia et al., 2009 suggest a concise typology of eWOM communications based on the level of user interactivity and participation; as such, they located these forms in a 2x2 framework as shown below. The authors suggest a framework that presents two dimensions, the type of communication (individual vs collective), and the level of interactivity (low vs high). This yielded four categories: many-to-one, one-to-many, many-to-many, and one-to-one represented in Figure 1.2 below.

Many-to-one or computer-by-computer is a collective kind of communication that represents the trend or preference of a crowd such as average ratings or votes. One-to-many is when an individual sends information to many others and when his level of interactivity is low. It requires the readers to exercise cognitive efforts to read the message; such is the case of product reviews. Many-to-many eWOM involves a lot of interaction in which consumers engage continuously in communication (i.e. discussion groups). Lastly, one-to-one eWOM is a private source of communication such as instant messaging. This typology not only represents the different types of eWOM, but also depicts how each type is processed by individuals. In this work, the main focus is the one-to-many eWOM since they represent the most widely available eWOM content on social network sites.

Electronic word of mouth can be classified into two main categories: primary and secondary information. Primary eWOM results from consumers' direct experiences while secondary eWOM is based on information they heard about from other sources (Hornik et al., 2015). These sources might include commercial material or other eWOM. Secondary

| | Low Interactivity | High Interactivity |
|---|---|---|
| Collective Communication | Many-to-one (computed by computer) | Many-to-many (highly involved) |
| Individual Communication | One-to-many (text based) | One-to-one (dyad based and private) |

*Figure 1.2* Types of eWOM communication (Adapted from Xia et al., 2009)

eWOM is particularly important since it is believed to compromise more than 70 percent of commercial eWOM (Meiners et al., 2010).

## Electronic word of mouth components

### How the sender *of the message may impact its reception offline and online*

The communicator is the person who transmits the communication. Traditional WOM emanates from a source that is generally known by the receiver; hence the credibility of the message and the sender are clear to the receiver. The literature on traditional WOM has proven that a personal source of information has an impact on consumer preferences and their choices (Arndt, 1967; Herr et al., 1991). In the offline context, people judge the sender based on several cues such as credibility, physical appearance, and familiarity. In the online context, consumers are not only confronted with communications emanating from their peers, but also those of people outside their social networks. They exchange information about goods and services with people dispersed geographically all over the planet through multiple online platforms (Davis & Khazanchi, 2008). This raises concerns about the credibility of the source, which constitutes the most studied element associated with the sender of the message. Source credibility refers to the perception the receiver has about the believability, competence, and trustworthiness of the communicator (Petty & Cacioppo, 1986). It includes two dimensions: trustworthiness and expertise. Other factors related to the communicator include attractiveness, disclosure of identity, shared geographical location, social ties, homophily, attribution, and social type. Attractiveness includes similarity, familiarity, and likability. It reflects a receiver's identification with the sender. Disclosure of identity is the act of exposing one's identity. Shared geographical location refers to people from the same area. Social ties represent the intensity of the relationship between individuals and finally, homophily is the degree of similarity between individuals.

### How the content *of the message is interpreted by the receivers*

The content of the eWOM message can take many forms. Research on the impact of eWOM can be divided into three categories: research that addresses the quantitative aspect of messages, those that focus on valence, and research that studies the qualitative attributes of messages. The quantitative aspect refers to the number of messages or, in general, to the amount of information conveyed by the message while the qualitative content can be understood through attributes specific to the quality of the message such as its objectivity, its accuracy, its usefulness, or its relevance. The valence as for it concerns the positive or negative aspect of the message. According to Bhattacherjee and Sanford (2006), quality is defined as the persuasive force of arguments. Argument quality is the persuasive strength of information. It includes relevance, timeliness, accuracy, and comprehensiveness (Bhattacherjee & Sanford, 2006). A large number of studies have demonstrated the impact of the quality of the arguments on the attitudes of the receivers, notably in a virtual environment (Zhang et al., 2014). If the arguments contained in the message are perceived as being of quality, then the receiver will adopt a positive attitude towards the message and perceive it as being credible (Cheung et al., 2009; Fan et al., 2013). Thus, the quality of a message on the Internet is measured through a multitude of criteria. According to the literature, the elements related to the message include argument quality, disconfirming information, eWOM credibility, argument strength, valence, consistency, rating, number of reviews, review type, visual cues, and dispersion. Disconfirming information refers to inconsistent information. eWOM credibility is the perceived ability of the truthfulness of a review. Argument strength is the extent to which a receiver views the message as being valid. Valence is whether the message is positive or negative. Consistency refers to the consistency with other reviews. Rating is the overall grade consumers give a review. Review type represents the orientation of a review. And finally, dispersion is the degree to which arguments differ from one person to the other.

*How the receiver's personal factors impact his interpretation of the message*

The receiver is the individual who receives and analyzes the content of a persuasive message. The impact of electronic communication varies according to personal judgment, which results in very distinct responses to recipients (Chaiken & Eagly, 1976). This depends, according to the literature, on a number of individual characteristics. Kallgren and Wood (1986) highlighted the difference in perceived risk levels between expert and novice users. Novice users are more easily influenced by extreme messages and quickly change their minds whereas expert users usually stay in their initial positions. Regarding expertise, Gilly et al. (1998) and Bansal and Voyer (2000) demonstrated that receiver expertise has a negative impact on the effect of WOM. Other individual factors have also been identified by the literature as moderators of the effect of an electronic communication. These are self-efficacy (Hsu et al., 2007), skepticism (Sher & Lee, 2009; Lee & Youn, 2009), familiarity (Munzel, 2015), expert opinion online (Park & Kim, 2008) or gender and social proximity (Ardelet, 2011). This difference in perception by the receivers of electronic communication has led researchers to look at the process of its adoption in order to understand the extent of the influence of the 58 messages. Sussman and Siegal (2003) have shown that the degree of knowledge and expertise of the receiver moderates the uptake of information across both central (argument quality) and peripheral (message subject) routes. Previous involvement and knowledge also play a significant role in controlling purchase intentions (Doh & Hwang, 2009; Park & Lee, 2008).

## *How the receiver reacts to the negative eWOM*

The response is a reaction from the receiver to persuasive communication. As previously reported, traditional word of mouth is considered to be a kind of social influence that affects consumers' beliefs, attitudes, and buying intentions (Ardent, 1967; Hanna & Wozniak, 2001). In the same way as its ancestor, the communication through the word of mouth influences a multitude of factors related to the attitude, the adoption of the information, the intention, and the behavior generally.

The adoption of the review is defined as the process by which individuals voluntarily commit to using information (Cheung et al., 2009; Sussman & Siegal, 2003). According to Lee and Koo (2012), this is the degree of acceptance of the message by the reader after evaluating its content. Moreover, Sussman and Siegal (2003) add that adoption is a construct that is intimately linked to the usefulness of the information contained in the notice, which reflects the informational influence of the latter. This implies that a consumer who adopts an opinion must accept the recommendations of the consumer, which is essentially a result of an action.

Negative eWOM can have a significant effect on other consumers shaping their purchasing behavior ergo impacting brands. These effects can range from not purchasing the product to actively seeking brand sabotage (Kahr et al., 2016). Of all the responses identified in the literature, purchase intent remains the most commonly studied.

Negative word of mouth has been through many changes over the years (Figure 1.3). It started with humans warning other humans about potential animalistic threats or hunting dangers on the Chauvet caves;

they then developed an oral rhetoric to persuade each other on the goodness and badness of different topics. With the rise of the Internet, people had a new outlet to generate negative online reviews about brands through eWOM. Finally, social network sites gave them a more personal setting to share this kind of information with their networks.

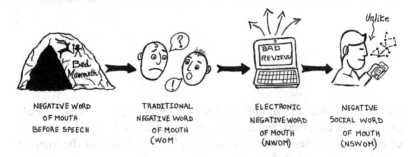

NEGATIVE WORD OF MOUTH BEFORE SPEECH

TRADITIONAL NEGATIVE WORD OF MOUTH (WOM)

ELECTRONIC NEGATIVE WORD OF MOUTH (NWOM)

NEGATIVE SOCIAL WORD OF MOUTH (NSWOM)

*Figure 1.3* The evolution of the negative word
Courtesy of Nayla Idriss

# 2 ... social media amplified the voice for WOM

Electronic word of mouth includes communication, which takes place on all kinds of digital platform, nevertheless, it mainly refers to communications occurring on review sites. The evolution of the Internet and the widespread plethora of new ways to exchange online have led to the need to distinguish a separate form of WOM: social eWOM (sWOM). Social eWOM refers to communication between individuals through social network sites. It has become one of the most frequently used eWOM (Chu & Kim, 2011). Compared to eWOM where posters are anonymous, sWOM presents several characteristics: the audience is intended (within the receiver's close network), information is more trusted, evaluation of the source is possible, interpersonal relationships are strong. This platform presents many opportunities for consumers and brands.

Previously, consumers had very few tools to voice out their complaints to organizations. Their only option was to individually address the brand, which might or might not yield the desired outcome. Consumers were unable to rally and bundle their objections. The rise of online sites, more specifically social network sites, has shifted power from companies to consumers (Hennig-Thurau et al., 2010). These complaints and negative talks about brands constitute negative word of mouth. Negative WOM occurring on social network sites is hereinafter referred to as NSWOM.

## From NWOM to NSWOM: when NWOM gets up close and social

### Social media vs social network sites

Before discussing the impacts of NSWOM, a brief review of academia is essential to understand the definition of social media, and their components.

The first objective is to elucidate the confusion surrounding the term social media. When tackling the social network sites, it is relevant to distinguish between social media and social network sites. Social media is defined as the platform on which individuals create, review, and share information with others. Social media can be considered as an umbrella that encompasses several platforms, which differ in technology but share the same goal: to facilitate interactions and information flow between users through a multiple-way communication exchange. Kaplan and Haenlein (2010) gave the following definition: "*A group of Internet-based applications that build on the ideological and technological foundations of Web 2.0, and that allows the creation and exchange of user-generated content.*"

The term social media combines communication and sociology. While the medium is a method of delivering or storing information (communication), social networks are structures composed of different actors reunited through complex dyadic ties (sociology) (Wasserman & Faust, 1994). Together, social media is a communication system allowing its users to communicate through dyadic ties.

Many perspectives have emerged on the classifications of social media; they are summarized in Table 2.1 below.

When tackling online media, it was noted that authors are often prone to have reductive or all-encompassing speeches due to the difficulty of distinguishing platforms that have distinctive characteristics within the set of social media. Evidently, how can we distinguish sites that appear to offer very different features? Thus, it is imperative to establish a clear and operational definition of social network sites (SNS).

Boyd and Ellison (2007) suggested a definition of social network sites that relatively captures their specificity. They define social network sites as:

web-based services that allow individuals to:

a. construct a public or semi-public profile within a bounded system,
b. articulate a list of other users with whom they share a connection,
c. view and transverse their list of connections and those made by others within the system.

The authors also oppose social network sites and social networking sites. The latter is focused on creating, developing, and maintaining a social network. Stenger and Coutant (2010) argue that this definition

*Table 2.1* Overview of social media categorization

| Social media classifications | Definitions |
| --- | --- |
| *Functionality vs unique usage* | This perspective is based on works of consultants and ecommerce practitioners. It entails two axes, the first one focuses on the **initial characteristics of the sites** (sharing sites, discussion sites, virtual worlds etc. ...). The second one relies on the **unique usage of the sites** (i.e. expression, socializing, games ...). |
| *Media characteristics vs self-representation* (Kaplan & Haenlein, 2010) | This perspective classifies social media based on two dimensions inspired by two theories: theory of social presence and the theory of media richness. ' **Self-presentation** refers to the desire of individuals to control the impressions others have of them. This can be achieved through **self-disclosure,** which is the conscious or unconscious disclosure of personal information. **Social presence/ media richness**: Social presence is influenced by the intimacy and the immediacy of the medium. Media richness theory is based on the assumption that the goal of every communication is the reduction of uncertainty. From this perspective, media channels differ in the amount of information that can be transmitted in a given period of time thus, differing in the resolution of ambiguity. The combination of these dimensions leads to the classification of social media into the following: *collaborative projects* (such as Wikipedia), *blogs and micro-blogs* (Twitter), *content communities* (such as YouTube), *virtual social worlds* (such as second life), *virtual game worlds* (such as World of Warcraft) and *social networking sites* (such as Facebook). |
| Cardon's cartography (2008) | It is based on two axes: <br> • Evaluating the exteriorization of identity by going from *being* to *doing.* <br> • Evaluating the distance between the *real identity* and the *projected one.* <br> Four categories of visibility emerge: civil identity, narrative identity, acting identity and virtual identity. |
| Digital youth project (Ito et al., 2010) | It distinguishes two kinds of participation: friendship driven online participation and interest driven online participation. |
| Stenger and Coutant's cartography (2013) | According to the authors it is imperative not to be limited by the functionalities offered by these platforms but rather grasp the functions that users have made of these sites. |

*Table 2.1* Cont.

| Social media classifications | Definitions |
|---|---|
| | They favor a **sociotechnical approach**, combining analysis of both the functionalities of the said sites and the *actual practices* that are made by the users. For instance, Facebook might structure its users' actions on its platform, however, they can resist, accept or refuse certain practices. The cartography is centered on two axes: participation and visibility. The first axis is based on Ito et al.'s (2010) friendship driven online participation versus the interest driven online participation. The second axis takes into account the sites' functionality and the practices made by its users while distinguishing the content based on what is made public. Thus, this axis opposes *self-representation* and *content publication*. |
| Four elements framework (Peters et al., 2013) | Authors describe four elements that make up social media and that interact and constantly reinforce each other: motives, content, network structure, and social roles and interactions. |

lacks a fourth fundamental element that separates SNS from social computation. They believe that individuals use SNS for no particular reason other than to create a profile and make it public through their interaction with other members. In other words, they seek to use their technical characteristics such as chatting, sharing pictures, etc., whereas their use of other sites such as Wikipedia and Youtube relies on obvious reasons; creating and sharing specific content. Therefore, they add the following element to the definition:

d. base their attractiveness essentially on the first three points and not on a particular activity.

When categorizing SNS, it is important to take into account their technical infrastructure. It's equally important to take into account the way these platforms are being used, but also their technical characteristics that will shape their future use. Nevertheless, a definition based on usage must be taken with precaution since usage can evolve with time. According to the authors, a social network is a breeding ground on which communities can emerge, but it does not merge with them. Thus, on Facebook, creating a profile, or accepting a friend will not constitute a mark of belonging to a community.

Even if a distinction has been made between social networking sites, virtual communities, and social network sites, it appears that, with time, these distinctions will no longer be of interest. Currently, Facebook gathers individuals in groups around a particular topic or interest. Many studies have noted these users feel a sense of belonging to a community (Zhang et al., 2012; Gummerus et al., 2012). Moreover, users are socializing and networking on this platform, add to it the fact Facebook is currently working on creating a dating functionality (Constine, 2019).

Social network sites are driven by user-generated content and aim at building and maintaining social networks. These sites can be public or private. Every individual is free to join these sites but he must register first. The specificity of these sites lies in the creation of a profile. Each individual creates a self-descriptive profile. This allows members to connect and interact with other members (Lampe et al., 2006). These connections are essential in social network sites as they constitute one of the most important reasons for spending time on these sites. These connections are named differently depending on the networks; they are often referred to as *friends* even though they differ in the level of social connections such as family members, colleagues, close friends, and celebrities (Boyd, 2006). They can be offline, online, or new connections (Dwyer et al., 2007; Lampe et al., 2006). They also differ in their nature as they can represent strong or weak ties (Ellison et al., 2007). Weak ties represent connections that may provide useful information to the recipient of the information, but don't necessarily have strong emotional support with them. Strong ties entail a robust connection between two individuals who share an emotional connection such as close friends or family (Granovetter, 1982). Social network sites encourage both kinds of ties (Ellison et al., 2007).

Social network sites are analyzed through social network analysis. Social network analysis is the study of social structures through network and graphs theory. Networks are analyzed in terms of nodes (the people or actors within a network) and ties (the relationships or links between the actors) that link them. One of the best known network theories is the six degrees of separation. It stipulates that two people are connected through only six degrees of separation (Barabasi, 2003). On Facebook, this separation has been reduced as users are separated by only three and a half connections (Bromwich, 2016).

The main objective of SNS is for people to communicate, build, and maintain relationships. Moreover, these sites not only allow people with the same interests to meet but also link people that would not have otherwise met who can bond over different topics. Consequently, users have formed dense network clusters (Wilson et al., 2009). These clusters make the information flow without restraints and constant, this means that a large number of people can be reached within a limited time frame (Pfeffer et al., 2014).

On SNS, brands have the same standing as any other actor in the network; they represent a node like any other. Consequently, these platforms are egalitarian by nature as opposed to other traditional media. The hierarchal structure is thus compromised. Consumers hold the same power as brands, if not more. These sites are mainly composed of user-generated content (UGC), not company-generated content. However, users are voluntarily exposed to marketing information (Chu & Kim, 2011).

Consumers are making new use of social networking sites (SNS) in a way that goes beyond socializing. Today, these messages consist of an exchange of information about goods and services. Consumers have become more empowered due to their access to instant information and their ability to interact with it promptly. In the case of content generation, consumers can spread eWOM very quickly to an unlimited number of people (King et al., 2014) at a fractional time frame. This content can impact a brand both positively and negatively. Moreover, people are resorting to SNS to get information about brands they are not acquainted with (Naylor et al., 2012) since information gathered through friends and personal networks is perceived as more credible (Chu & Kim, 2011). The negative information they might find on SNS can, therefore, be very influential.

One of the biggest challenges for brands on SNS is the ability of these sites to spread rumors quickly. Whereas hubs share the information with a big audience, average users are quick to share the information with their neighbors. Surprisingly, Doer et al. (2012) found that nodes with fewer neighbors had a larger propensity to quickly disseminate rumors.

## NSWOM across platforms

In terms of the content of NSWOM, it has already been established that it can relate a product/service failure or a value-based failure. As for the form of NSWOM, it varies between:

- Discussions about the product or service in private messages with friends.
- Discussions about the product or service on the brand's public page with friends or strangers.

• Commenting on other users' status updates.
• Creating a post about a brand and posting it on social platforms.
• Sharing a post about a brand (a friends' post or an online article).
• Checking-in at the brand's location.

As for the message characteristics of NSWOM, every message can be defined in terms of its cognitive and affective characteristics (Yap et al., 2013). These characteristics affect the persuasiveness of a message (Sweeney et al., 2012; Mazzarol et al., 2007). While the cognitive message characteristics represent the "what you're saying," the affective message characteristics represents the "how you say it." Affective message characteristics refer to the depth, vividness, and intensity of the way a message is conveyed. It indicates the nature of the language used, and the extent of storytelling in the message (Mazzarol et al., 2007; Sweeney et al., 2012). There are many factors that compose affective message characteristics for NSWOM such as the emotionally charged language used by the sender of the message, the use of aggressive or extensive punctuation marks (i.e. use of exclamation marks), the use of graphical content (i.e. pictures and videos), and the use of expressive emoticons. Folse et al. (2016) qualify them as negatively valanced emotional expressions (NVEE) that include exclamation points, all caps, emoticons and intense language.

How is information diffusion facilitated across SNS? An overview of the most popular SNS will shed light on this matter. The SNS that have the most active users are Facebook (2.234 billion users), Instagram (1 billion), Twitter (335 million), and SnapChat (291 million) (Hervé, 2019). The main characteristics of each SNS and its effects on NSWOM are presented in Table 2.2.

Facebook offers many specificities that make it ideal for NSWOM propagation. Concerning the nature of the network of users on Facebook it's described as a network of friends, if a person A is friends with person B, the latter is automatically friends with A. The average (mean) number of friends is 338 (Brandwatch, 2019). In a month, the average user likes ten posts, makes four comments, and clicks on eight ads (Brandwatch, 2019).

Unlike other SNS, Facebook encourages openness by showing a person's affiliation for groups of interest and stresses the disclosure of the user's real identity (Kim et al., 2018). Facebook's algorithms help connect people who might know each other in real life, but are not necessarily connected online, which provides more informational reach. Moreover, they will suggest brands and groups for users to join based on their interests and the information they provided on the platform. Even

*Table 2.2* Characteristics of main social network sites

| SNS platform | Main functionalities | Nature of NSWOM | Effects on NSWOM |
|---|---|---|---|
| Facebook | • **Post types:** Long form content (texts, pictures, videos, links and ephemeral stories that disappear in 24 hours) <br> • **Characters limits:** No limit <br> • **Activities:** Create extensive profile, browse a tailored newsfeed, search for information, join groups, follow brands, create and share content, like and comment posts, chat privately, buy products. | • Creating posts <br> • Sharing other people's posts <br> • Checking-in <br> • Joining/creating brand opposing groups <br> • Reacting negatively to brands' posts (angry face) | • The most exhaustive of SNS in terms of functionalities. <br> • The profile is based on user's true identity that increases credibility of NSWOM. |
| Instagram | • **Post types:** Filtered videos and pictures with caption and ephemeral stories that disappear in 24 hours. <br> • **Characters limits:** No limits. <br> • **Activities:** Post and share pictures and stories, browse friends feed, like and comment posts, follow brands, chat privately, buy products. | • Creating posts <br> • Sharing other people's posts <br> • Checking-in <br> • Creating/ spreading viral hashtags | • The platform creates gaps in information dissemination. <br> • It's more focused on visual content. <br> • It's optimized for mobile viewing not intuitive on computer formats. |
| Twitter | • **Post types:** Short form messages (text, picture, video, links). | • Creating posts | • The platform is very high paced, it might be hard to keep track of a negative Tweet. |

*(continued)*

*Table 2.2* Cont.

| SNS platform | Main functionalities | Nature of NSWOM | Effects on NSWOM |
|---|---|---|---|
| | • **Characters limits:** 280 characters.<br>• **Activities:** Browse topics through #, create and share content, like and comment posts, follow brands, chat privately. | • Sharing other people's posts (retweeting)<br>• Checking-in<br>• Creating/ spreading viral hashtags | • Many users use a username and not their real names, which questions the concept of source credibility. |
| Snapchat | • **Post types:** Visual form content (pictures and videos shared are deleted after 24 hours)<br>• **Characters limits:** No limits<br>• **Activities:** browse content, create and share content, chat privately (chats are also deleted with 24 hours). | • Taking pictures/ videos<br>• Sending pictures/ videos | • The disappearing content makes it hard to keep track of information.<br>• The platform does not allow for much exchange between different members. |

though interest has decreased among young people towards Facebook as their parents have joined the platform (Dreyfuss et al., 2019) and the rise of social media fatigue has started (Bright et al., 2015). The site has strived to regain its younger users by updating its features and including "stories" that disappear within 24 hours. Nevertheless, it remains the most used platform and the most ideal one for sharing and finding product-related information (Aghakhani et al., 2016).

Instagram is a network of followers, if a person A is friends with person B, the latter can choose whether or not to be friends with A. Over 95 million photos are uploaded each day (Brandwatch, 2019). The platform encourages WOM diffusion by enticing people to tag their friends on different posts and inviting them to check brand or peer content (Latiff et al., 2015). The use of hashtags promotes the quantification of attention; it makes it easier for users to find a topic of interest and to follow up on trending topics notably recent brand crises.

Twitter is a network of information or peers; users can follow a person without having to be followed back. It's an oriented graph social network. Information diffusion is faster and simpler on Twitter. A rumor starting at a random node can reach 4.5 million of its total of 51.5 million members in just eight cycles of communication (Doer et al., 2012). There are 500 million Tweets sent each day, which is equivalent to 6000 Tweets per second (Brandwatch, 2020).

Snapchat is an ephemeral social network where content is auto-deleted after a limited time (Wakefield & Bennett, 2018). This ephemeral feature was so successful it was replicated by Facebook and Instagram in their "Stories" functionality. Text, photos, and videos sent on Snapchat are easily viewed and disappear once they're read or viewed. Snapchat is a network of friends. It has over 160 million daily active users (Constine, 2017). Over 2 million snaps are sent every minute (Brandwatch, 2019).

## The drastic consequences of NSWOM: depicting negative consumer behavior

### Why is NSWOM so important for brands?

NSWOM constitutes a threat for brands because they can't control how it's created or how it's shared. Previously, marketers were in complete control of their communications and the way they wanted consumers to perceive their brands. They controlled the length, reach, valence, and the timing of these communications (Wakefield & Bennett, 2018). Consumers were limited by these messages since they didn't have access to alternate information. Nevertheless, the rise of social media has significantly altered the power shift in communication (Berger, 2014). Marketers are now at the mercy of their followers who will decide whether to post positive or negative information about them.

The reach and speed of information diffusion on SNS is another challenge for marketers in terms of NSWOM. Digital messages can reach an unlimited number of people in a very limited time. Moreover, they can be shared and picked up instantly (Hansen et al., 2018). It is therefore nearly impossible to stop NSWOM if it's detected too late. This ease of spread enables users to reach a large number of potential consumers in little time and inform them of the brand's wrongdoings by co-creating and sharing brand-related information (Labrecque et al., 2013). Consumers have real-time access to a large number of friends (Hennig-Thurau et al., 2015); therefore, consumer exposure to NSWOM is accelerated and intensified. Moreover, research shows that people find messages charged with negative emotions such as anger are more credible than positive word of mouth (Berger & Miklkman, 2012), which makes NSWOM more likely to diffuse more quickly and more widely. Studies have also shown that NWOM impacts consumer behavior and attitudes (Park & Lee, 2009; Chevalier & Mayzlin, 2006).

Besides the impact NSWOM has on individuals and consumers, the effect on companies is also significant, notably in terms of brand perceptions and reputation, but also on the company's bottom line as well as the spillover into other brands. Both professional and academic studies have shown examples of negative brand perceptions following the dissemination of NSWOM. They have demonstrated how negative sentiment expressed through SNS can lead to a brand crisis, which can cause a significant loss of consumers as well as considerable damage to the brand's reputation (Hennig-Thurau et al., 2010; Pfeffer et al., 2014). The impact on a brand's reputation can ultimately impact the company's bottom line. Once consumers perceive the brand differently, they will refrain from buying its products, which will impact a firm's revenue (Kim et al., 2016) and stock values (Tirunillai & Tellis, 2012).

One of the first NWOM tackled in the literature is the "Dell Hell" (Jarvis, 2005). That year, a blogger related his negative experience with Dell's customer service. It was only a matter of hours before other people read the post and joined him in sharing their own disappointing experiences with the brand. This ripple effect was the main factor that led to a decrease in Dell's customer satisfaction rating as well as a decrease in the stock price (Furfie, 2008). In another example, United Airlines broke Dave Carroll's guitar. He got so angry at the company for handling the situation poorly and not answering him that he produced the song "United Breaks Guitars" and posted it on YouTube. The video has been viewed by over 20 million individuals and the damages caused are estimated at 180$ million (*The Economist*, 2009). To this day, people are still using #UnitedBreaksGuitars whenever the airlines mess up.

Some companies view these brand crisis as a risk to their reputation while others compare social media outrage to "*a beast with the fangs of a rattlesnake, and the attention span of a gnat*" (Knowledge@Wharton, 2015), meaning social media gives the illusion that the outrage is more dangerous and risky than it really is.

Moreover, the brands that are the subject of the NSWOM are not the only brands that are affected by these communications, other brands that provide similar products/services can also be impacted, which is why it's crucial for brands to carefully monitor NSWOM in their industries. Studies have shown that the *perverse halo* or *negative spillover*, which is defined as the phenomenon whereby the negative talks about one brand can negatively impact the talks of another brand offering the

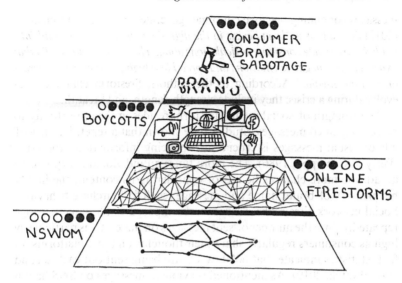

*Figure 2.1* The escalation of NSWOM
Courtesy Nayla Idriss

same products, exists. While studying the NSWOM during a car recall,
Borah and Tellis (2016) found that these negative effects spill over onto
other car models.

## The escalation of NSWOM: online firestorms, boycott, and sabotage

While it's true that one negative comment about a brand will not have
an immediate and direct impact on the company's sales, the escalation
and the repetition of such posts can lead to bigger and harder to control phenomena such as (by order of seriousness): online firestorms,
boycotts or even brand sabotage (Figure 2.1).

### Online firestorms: information diffusion similar to epidemics

The sudden occurrence of many NSWOM against brand results in
online brand crises or social media firestorms. Social media firestorm
differs from other digital crisis due to these site's specificities. Such
specificities include extreme dynamics that make social media firestorms
grow exponentially in a short period of time (Hansen et al., 2018).

The idea of a social media firestorm was introduced by Pfeffer et al.
(2014). The authors define social media firestorms as large quantities of

messages containing negative consumer-generated content. Hansen et al. (2018) define it as a *"brand crisis in the digital age that consist of multiple, publicly observable consumer articulations about a brand on social media that express strong negative emotions and spread in a highly dynamic way across and within media."* According to the authors, firestorm characteristics evolve during a crisis: they include strength, length, and breadth.

The strength of social media firestorm resides in the opportunity to present repeated messages. Studies have shown that a repetitive view of ads or visual messages is crucial in enhancing information processing (Petty & Cacioppo, 1986). The more times an individual is exposed to an ad, the more chances he has of considering its content, the higher his memory of brand name and message recall for purchase behaviors. Social network sites make it easier to be exposed to the same message repeatedly since the number of sent messages on these sites is particularly high as consumers regularly share their thoughts on these platforms. In fact, statistics indicate that 6000 tweets are being sent out each second (Brandwatch, 2019). As mentioned previously, messages on SNS have a high reach and speed, which increases not only the possibility for consumers to send messages, but also for them to encounter it. The more chances consumers have of being exposed to the negative message, the higher the likelihood of them processing the information relating to the brand crisis (Hansen et al., 2018).

Some social media firestorms pop up and vanish within days, while others last much longer, giving SNS users the time to let the information sink in and set in their memory. The length of exposure to a message is relevant in determining a negative message's effectiveness. Studies in advertising have shown that the length of exposure to an ad can have a positive impact; repeated ads enhance processing and make brands more credible (Hawkins & Hoch, 1992). Similarly, it can be expected that repeated exposure to NSWOM would yield the same results. Thus, the longer a crisis or NWOM lasts on SNS, the more consumers will be exposed to it and process it, which leads to longer-lasting negative effects such as bad brand perception.

Finally, the breadth of social media firestorms refers to the number of media outlets, both print and digital, that also tackle the issue. This added occurrence of the negative information should enhance repetition in the consumer's mind, thus allowing them to process the negative message further. These media outlets might provide additional information on a certain brand crisis that SNS fail to provide due to space or other platform restrictions (such as Twitter's 280 characters restrictions). Consumers can form a more comprehensive approach to the subject matter. In the pre-digital age, crisis were known to spread only through mass media, such as television, newspapers, and radio, and occasionally through consumer protests or manifestation. Social media granted consumers the power to articulate themselves subjectively whereas they used to rely on official media sources previously (Labrecque et al., 2013). Drasch et al. (2015) compare the spread of negative information diffusion to that of an epidemic. In both information diffusion and epidemiology, the disease characteristics, as well as the structure of the network, play a part in their transmission. NSWOM, just like pathogenic organisms, can propagate through (online) social links among SNS users. Therefore, the infection rate depends on the negative information (its valence and transmission complexity), network structure (density and interconnectedness), and the information attaining process through the network. Moreover, similar to the early detection of a disease, the early detection of an online firestorm can be detrimental in eliminating it.

NSWOM turned to social media firestorms that can evolve into an active consumer aggressive behavior that can be instrumental (boycotts) or hostile (brand sabotage).

## Boycotts, an instrumental aggression

The phenomenon of anti-consumption has received a lot of attention in recent years (Lee & al., 2009). As its name implies, anti-consumption refers to actions focused against consumption. It encompasses reductions of consumptions as well as non-consumptions, but can also be specific to some brands or products (Kozinets et al., 2010; Iyer & Muncy, 2008). It has been studied through different approaches (Lee et al., 2009; Kavaliauskė & Simanaviciute, 2015) seeing it can take different forms, which include boycotts (Friedman, 1985; Farah & Newman, 2010), brand avoidance (Lee et al., 2009), ethical consumption (Carrigan & Atalla, 2001), brand rejection (Wheeler et al., 2013), and consumer resistance (Lee et al., 2011).

A boycott is a form of anti-consumption behavior whereby market activists refrain from purchasing a product or service to obtain objectives (Friedman, 1985). It represents an important element of consumer complaint behavior as it suggests a response from consumers to a company's offerings (Singh, 1988). Consumer boycotts are targeted at specific brands and have a defined objective (Hoffmann, 2011).

Many reasons trigger a boycott campaign such as social, political, ethical, environmental, religious, and so on. These campaigns are increasing as the general market trend is leaning towards a favorable corporate social responsibility. Individuals will resort to such behavior when they feel that their well-being or that of their society is being threatened by unappropriate behavior (Friedman, 1999). It's aimed at increasing the good of all by modifying company behavior and practices that are deemed to compromise that welfare (Yuksel, 2013). This is why some boycotts can be viewed as a prosocial behavior where the end result is aimed at benefiting people beyond one's self (Klein et al., 2004).

The motivations behind taking part in online boycott are twofold: instrumental, and non-instrumental motivations. Boycotts driven by instrumental motivations have clearly stated claims and objectives, the behavior of the boycotters is put forth to influence an explicit change in company policies (Friedman, 1999). Sometimes individuals join boycotts for non-instrumental motivations such as expressive boycotts, where boycotters are usually venting out their feelings and expressing themselves (Friedman, 1999). According to psychological reasons, individuals would resort to expressive boycott as a means to reduce their frustrations, thus, experiencing relief. Another non-instrumental boycott is motivated by self-enhancement reasons where individuals would participate only to enhance their self-esteem or free themselves of the moral obligation and feeling of guilt (Klein et al., 2004).

Marketing studies have explored the role of emotions and their impact on consumer behavior (Bagozzi et al., 1999). The role of emotions is all the more important in an anti-consumption context. Emotions play a crucial part in consumer boycotts, in fact, previous work has stated that boycott participation is an emotional expression of a customer's attitude (Farah & Newman, 2010). This is particularly true for boycotts that have non-instrumental motivations (Klein et al., 2002).

Needless to say, boycotts impact brands negatively. They negatively influence consumer attitudes and purchase intentions (Makarem & Jae, 2016) as well as the brand image (Klein, 2004). Studies on the effects of boycotts on the company's bottom line remain unsettled, however, many works have shown that boycott campaigns can lead to drops in stock price (Pruitt & Friedman, 1986) as well as changes in company policies (Davidson et al., 1995).

The mere threat or announcement of a boycott is enough to impact a company before it has actually begun. In June 2020, many brands decided to protest Facebook's hate-speech policies by the boycotting Facebook ads through the month of July. Shares of the company fell 8.3 percent a few days before the beginning of July, costing the company a $7 billion loss.

*Brand sabotage, a hostile aggression*

Whereas NSWOM, online firestorms, and boycotts constitute a threat to brands, which does not necessarily arise from an intentional motive to hurt them directly (but rather a means to obtain different objectives, such as restoring equity), brand sabotage represents intended hostile aggression towards the brand.

Originally, the term sabotage comes from the French word *sabot*, which is a wooden clog that angry workers tossed in the machines during the French Revolution as a sign of distort and with a purpose to harm their companies. Consumer brand sabotage is deliberate hostile aggression, by consumers or non-consumers, whose objective is to harm the brand through impairing brand associations for other consumers (Kahr et al., 2016). At this point, the relationship between the consumer and the brand is broken beyond repair.

Consumer brand sabotage is an intentional and deliberate act. The actions taken within this scope are carefully planned and chosen due to their potential to cause harm to the brand, they are not impulsive, automatic responses such as sharing a message on SNS (NSWOM). Saboteurs exert a lot of effort and spend significant time to figure out how to successfully cause harm to a brand and distort its perceptions in other consumers' minds. This behavior is only achieved once the harm takes place. Therefore, imagining the possible ways one can hurt the brand does not constitute brand sabotage, the actual action is required. This action can take place online or offline or both. There is no unified description of an activity that automatically qualifies as brand sabotage (Kahr et al., 2016), it can vary from creating a video that attacks the brand to using social media to spread misappropriations of the brands' original logo. In a nutshell, it can be any activity where the main motive is to cause harm to the brand. The latter is the main target for saboteurs as it represents a valuable company asset. The Davis Carrol example stated earlier spiraled into an online firestorm. When people shared his video, it constituted NSWOM. However, David's individual action is a brand sabotage behavior.

# 3 People started talking negatively about brands on SNS ...

Studying the influence of user-generated content, especially negative content, is essential because it underlines consumer influence within the marketplace (Riegner, 2007) and the challenge brands are faced with the challenge of controlling it. Marketers need to understand what motivates followers to create negative brand-related content on these platforms and how it influences what they talk about and product choices by other consumers (Yayli & Bayram, 2012) to craft adequate response strategies.

It's true that NSWOM can tarnish the reputation of brands, but is that all it does? How does it impact the behavior of its writer? This impact has been overlooked in the literature as many works have focused on the impacts of NSWOM on the receiver. To get a better understanding of what goes on in the sender's mind, it's relevant to apprehend the consumer decision journey and how it has shifted over the years.

## Consumer decision journey and the ZMOT

To better understand *why* individuals share NSWOM, it is relevant to go through the customer decision journey to get a better grasp of the context in which they decide to share such information.

Word of mouth has a strong influence on several stages of the consumer decision process (De Bruyn & Lilien, 2008). It even goes beyond the decision-making process to include consumer expectations, pre-usage attitudes (Herr et al., 1991) and post-usage perceptions (Bone, 1995). Traditionally, the consumer decision journey process consisted of five stages: need recognition, information search, evaluation, purchase, and post-purchase (Engel et al., 1993). Once the consumer identifies a need, he will initiate an information search to gather data about the product or service he wishes to obtain. He will resort to both internal (memory) as well as external (online research, friends' opinions ...)

sources of information. He will then evaluate his options by comparing and weighing up the alternatives. Finally, he will make the purchasing decision. If his experience is satisfactory with the product or service, he will consider buying it again, if not; he will refrain from doing so. In this case, he would resort to NWOM to narrate this experience.

Similar to the traditional word of mouth, previous research has proved that electronic word of mouth impacts the consumer's decision-making process regarding purchase (Cheung et al., 2009). This impact is evident in each one of the stages of the decision-making process. However, a study by McKinsey (Court et al., 2009) found that the traditional linear customer decision journey model is no longer relevant as eWOM has altered the way individuals gather information along the way to making purchasing decisions. Instead, they suggest that the decision journey has become a continuous loop where consumers keep adding and subtracting brands from their consideration set as they gather information from their online peers. Moreover, Endelman (2010) extended the post-purchase stage by adding the loyalty loop, which includes a positive behavior towards the brand: enjoy, advocate, and bond. A few years later, this model was revised (Court et al., 2017) as it was suggested that loyalty was hard to achieve when consumers are constantly exposed to different brands while they *shop around* having been subject to their friends' opinions on SNS and want to consider what works for them and what doesn't work. Authors advise marketers to focus on attracting consumers early on in their journey. It is suggested that consumers constantly make associations about brands, positive or negative, at all stages of the decision journey. A negative review on Facebook, a check-in with an emoticon, a frustrating experience with a website, all these are factors in the consumer's brand perceptions. Detecting these negative perceptions at an early stage can help brands be proactive.

Applying the consumer decision journey on SNS would be illustrated as follows. External stimuli such as peer reviews or messages on SNS can entice an individual's need recognition for a certain product. Imagine Sophie is scrolling through her Facebook feed, she comes across a picture Carol posted raving about her new Maybelline eyeliner. Sophie takes a moment to read the caption accompanying the post and realizes she too, needs new eyeliner. She then starts researching eyeliners online and visits Maybelline's site as well as their social pages. She reads people's comments on the pages and she checks their products. She notices one of her other friends, Cindy, has posted on the company page claiming the new eyeliner she bought was not as long-lasting as advertised and demanded a refund. Sophie now has mixed reviews, so she decides to conduct more research to compare possible alternatives before making a decision. She finally decides to make the purchase since she liked the way the brand responded to the negative feedback they got. She makes the purchase on the company website. Her experience with the product will determine what she does next. Once she tries the eyeliner, she might enjoy it or not be satisfied with it. In the former, she can choose to like/follow Maybelline's social pages, comment on a picture of the product or even create a post about her *"satisfying new find,"* she can also stop at talking about it with her friends; in other words, instigating positive word of mouth. However, if the product does not meet her expectations, she might feel confused (cognitive dissonance) and resort to social network sites to narrate her experience, give the product a bad rating, and spread NSWOM.

The stage where Sophie started researching eyeliners is called the *Zero Moment of Truth* (ZMOT). In 2005, Procter & Gamble first came up with the term *First Moment of Truth* (FMOT) to describe the consumer's first interaction with a company's product, be it on the shelf or when they first see it online. With the rise of the Internet and the increased use of search engines, the first encounter between a brand and the potential consumer was no longer the first moment the latter *sees* the product, but the moment he learns more about it as he gathers more information online (Lecinski, 2011), the zero moment of truth (ZMOT). The second moment of truth represents the moment the consumer experiences the product. Some authors talk about a third moment of truth, where the consumer talks about his (good or bad) experience with the product.

The ZMOT is an important stage when consumers are confronted with NSWOM. The information generated by their peers on their social media outlets will have an impact on how they will perceive the brand and their reactions[1] as one person's second moment of truth becomes another person's ZMOT. The process is depicted in Figure 3.1 below.

## Why do people instigate NSWOM?

Before discussing the motivations behind instigating NSWOM, it is essential to distinguish between two kinds of NSWOM: creating NEWSOM and sharing NSWOM. As previously stated, NSWOM can either be the result of a negative encounter with the brand where the individual would *create* a post about the said experience; or the result of relating or *sharing* the NSWOM of another individual on social network sites.

The first kind usually entails that the sender of this message has personally encountered an unsatisfactory experience with the brand. The NSWOM will result directly from this experience; the consumer will

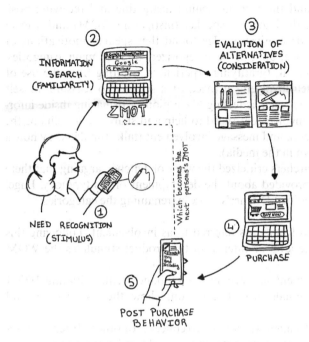

*Figure 3.1* The consumer decision journey on SNS
Courtesy of Nayla Idriss

create a message, post a picture, or share a link while adding a personal comment. However, in some cases, the writer of the message is not an actual consumer, but someone who is deeply touched by the negative company's actions, to the point that he's intrinsically motivated to create content about the incident. The second kind involves a secondary NSWOM where the transmitter is a receiver of the negative message, he adheres to the message for its content or the nature of the relationship he has with the sender thus, he will share this message to help spread the information. However, he is not the original creator of the content.[2]

Creating NSWOM is therefore powered by several motivations. Before the Internet, a lot of academic work has tackled the motivations behind engaging in WOM. Anderson (1998) found that consumers engage in WOM when their consumption expectations are not met. While Sundaram et al. (1998) suggested that motives for positive WOM are different than for negative WOM. One of the earliest works on WOM is that of Dichter (1966), published in the *Harvard Business Review*. Dichter conducted in-depth interviews with 255 consumers to better understand the reasons behind instigating and receiving positive WOM. He distinguishes speaker (instigating WOM) and listener (receiving WOM) motivation. He found that speaker motivations of WOM communication can be categorized in four main categories: product involvement (gratifying experiences resulting from the use of the product), self-involvement (need of a speaker to reassure himself in front of others, such as feeling like a pioneer or having inside information), other involvement (need to help and share the benefits of the product to others), and message involvement (talk stimulated by how a product is shown in the media).

Several researchers criticized the work of Ditcher, arguing that there are no details provided about the development of his typology. Engel et al. (1993) modified Ditcher's work by renaming the categories:

1.  Product involvement is referred to as involvement. Following this concept, the level of interest in the product stimulates the WOM discussion.
2.  Self-involvement has become self-enhancement. Initiating WOM helps individuals attract attention; show their know-how and superiority.
3.  Other involvement was altered to concern for others. It represents a genuine desire to help others make good purchasing decisions.
4.  Message involvement changed to message intrigue. It refers to the entertaining value of talking about ads.

They also added a new motivation, *dissonance reduction*, which they believe to be explanatory to negative WOM. However, the most exhaustive work on WOM motivation was that of Sundaram et al. (1998). They carried out 390 critical incident interviews. Their findings validate previous work of Dichter and Engel but also build on it to provide additional motives for instigating negative WOM. Sundaram et al. (1998) identify four categories that explain motivations behind positive WOM communication: altruism, product involvement, self-enhancement, and helping the company. They also identified four categories that explain negative WOM communication: anxiety reduction (reducing frustration), altruism (help others avoid negative experiences arising from similar problems), vengeance (retaliate after a negative consumption experience), and advice-seeking (getting advice on how to solve a problem).

Given the conceptual closeness of eWOM and traditional WOM communication, consumer motives that have been identified in the literature as being relevant for traditional WOM also can be expected to be of relevance for eWOM (Hennig-Thurau et al., 2004). These motivations are discussed more thoroughly, taking into account SNS specificities in what follows. The reasons why consumers engage in NSWOM are numerous. A thorough scrutiny of the literature has led to the detection of the following categories individual, social, and situational factors. Naturally, a single NSWOM communication can be motivated by the combination of several of these factors.

## Individual factors as a drive for NSWOM

The difference between spreading negative word of mouth face to face and doing so on social network sites is the perceived risks associated with different characteristics of NSWOM; this communication will last far beyond an oral discussion. Therefore, one has to be fully motivated to partake in this act, which should allow him to achieve individual benefits. These benefits would include factors that add value to the sender's self-image, his emotions, or his quest for knowledge. They include impression management (Berger, 2014), emotion regulation (Amblee & Biu, 2008), and damage repair (Zaraket, 2019).

*Impression management*

The marketing literature is abundant with references linking the consumption of certain products with social aspirations. Social interactions are for the large part, a performance where people tend to present the version of themselves that would achieve favorable impressions or a projection of who they want to be while hiding signals that would communicate undesired impressions (Belk, 1988; Berger et al., 2014). In the luxury industry, for example, studies show that people consume these products to boost their self-esteem (Belk, 1988), express their identity, and show status. These possessions signal relevant information to others about how these people wish to be perceived (Richins, 1994). The impression people make on others is key in this example; they would buy lavish goods to communicate a desired level of prestige. Similarly, people share WOM to control the image others make of them, or possibly the desired image they wish to convey (Berger et al., 2014). In the case of NSWOM, this impression manifests through self-enhancement and face concern. Self-enhancement is an essential human motivation (Fiske, 2001). It's natural for individuals to present themselves in the best light to gain desired impressions. Face concern encompasses the human need for social acceptance (Brown & Levinson, 1987). It refers to the desired projection of self-worth to others; it represents the extent to which individuals care about the protection of face. Instinctively, face concern depends on others to exist, thus, it can be gained, maintained, and lost through social interactions (Wan et al., 2016). People with high face concerns are more likely to have higher cognitive dissonance from the chance of losing face, which is why they would resort to NSWOM. They are also more likely to use facework strategies such as emotions expression and aggressive behavior that helps them maintain a reliable and conflict winning image to others (Balaji et al., 2016).

How does face concern impact *how* consumers create NSWOM? Individuals with high face concern will most likely distort the story to make it more interesting when consumers are resorting to NSWOM to enhance the entertaining impression in other user's minds, they might tend to exaggerate the way they report the experience, just as seen with the rumor diffusion process. Moreover, studies have indicated that people exaggerate when telling stories for entertaining purposes (Burrus et al., 1996).

How does face concern impact *what* consumers choose to talk about? Evidently, consumers will only share things that paint them in the best light (Chung & Darke, 2006). In the NSWOM context, SNS users would talk about product/service failures that would make them appear as *intelligent shoppers* (Sundaram et al., 1998) and brand value-based failures that make them appear as empathetic and considerate to social, environmental, or ethical issues.

Beyond projecting the desired image of one's self, people seek to communicate information that indicates particular identities (Packard & Wooten, 2013). Many active SNS users wish to become *the* source of information on specific subjects. Consumers who often talk about technology news want others to portray them as technical wizards; they would resort to NSWOM to signal expertise in the domain. Also, activists engage in NSWOM to show their adherence to a cause by letting their peers know about their support. Their act is motivated by a need to express certain parts of their identity whether it's being a supporter of human rights or an active fighter for global warming or an ally for the Black Lives Matter movement.

How does expressing one's identity impact *what* consumers create NSWOM? To seem smarter, people will post useful information. Product recalls are the most common manifestation of this purpose. What makes you seem more helpful and smart than telling your peers that the herbal supplement Kratom they love so much isn't as organic as they think, rather, it contains opioids and traces of salmonella that can lead to overdose, and potentially, death? Self-enhancement theories suggest that people would rather share positive information than negative because it makes them look better (Chevalier & Mayzlin, 2006). Evidently, when consumers make good consumption choices, it reflects on them, when they talk about the amazing new smartphone they got it shows they are just as amazing to have made this discovery. However, the opposite is true, they will perceive their bad choices as a reflection of them, which is why they'd be reluctant to post negative information. Nevertheless, when the role of the sender is taken out of the equation, people are more inclined to share negative information, which is why value-based brand failures are shared more easily. Individuals signaling their support to a cause will talk about these failures.

*Emotion regulation*

The second self-oriented antecedent to NSWOM is emotion regulation. Emotion regulation is the process by which individuals try to control their emotions to achieve desired outcomes. It dictates which emotions manifest themselves, when they appear, and how individuals express them (Gross, 2008). People can mainly manage their emotions in two ways: altering the assessment of the external stimulus (reappraisal) or changing the internal cue that triggered the behavioral response (emotion suppression) (Gross, 2008). Engaging in NSWOM helps consumers regulate their emotions by seeking social support, revenge, venting, and reducing dissonance.

According to the social support theory, people rely on support that others give in their social network to cope with stress (Cohen & Wills, 1985). Following a negative experience with a brand, people can resort to NSWOM to seek comfort and consolation from their network (Rimé, 2007). This would help attenuate negative feelings arising from the dissatisfactory experience. A person's perceived available social support is more important than the actual support he receives since it enhances his well-being by shielding him during stressful events.

Social support is determined through different network characteristics (Balaji et al., 2016): the structure of the social network (size), the belief about members (relative to their support in bad times), and their actions. These factors would determine how much an individual will rely on the network for social support and ultimately how likely he is to instigate NSWOM.

On the other hand, NSWOM can entice a vengeful behavior from consumers. Previous research has shown that dissatisfaction can result in consumers holding a grudge against the company, which in turn can result in seeking revenge by avoiding all interactions with the firm (McCullough et al., 2001). The desire for revenge or the consumer's will to punish the brand implies a desire to harm the brand (Bechwati & Morrin, 2003). Such behaviors are aligned with consumer brand sabotage (Kahr et al., 2016). This act of punishing the company regulates consumer's emotions. While seeking revenge is similar to venting, the former's main goal is to restore equity while the latter's objective is to enhance consumer's feelings.

Research has shown that consumers vent out their dissatisfaction when faced with a negative experience for many reasons, among which is to get a sense of relief (De Matos, 2008). Sharing frustration about the cancellation of a hit Netflix series provides catharsis and reduces emotional tension (Berger, 2014). The mere act of talking about upsetting subjects helps regulate one's emotions.

Upon going through an unsatisfying experience, consumers will experience cognitive dissonance that violates the psychological contract of his relationship with the company, thus, they will resort to NSWOM to reduce this dissonance (Ng et al., 2011). Talking to others may help to reassure them that they've made the right decision and reduces feelings of doubt (Engel et al., 1993).

How does emotion regulation impact *what* consumers choose to talk about? Psychological studies on social sharing argue that people share up to 90 percent of their emotional experiences with others (Walker et al., 2009). Moreover, studies have proved that arousal increases social transmission (Berger & Milkman, 2012). Consumers are therefore more likely to engage in NSWOM with high negative arousal or strong emotions such as anger and disgust.

### Damage repair

SNS users are aware that they can exercise a certain power over brands. They think of SNS as a place where they can have conversations with brands. Thus, in the case of brand failure, they would use the means allocated to them by the site to retrieve their rights or compensations. They resort to expressing their disappointment with the brand on its fan page or calling them out by tagging them in a comment on their own wall in hopes of getting a remedy or seeking damage repair. Many companies' customer services take an extended period of time to get back to customers, which is why they resort to the brand's social pages to pressure them into giving a prompt response.

## Social factors as a drive for NSWOM

NSWOM is not only driven by self-oriented motivation, but also by altruistic incentives. These incentives include bonding, warning, and informing others.

### Bonding with others

According to Dunbar's social bonding theory (1998), talking serves a bonding function. Interpersonal communication fills the need for social interaction (Hennig-Thurau et al., 2004). NSWOM helps to bond through reinforcing shared views. Talking to peers about brands that have failed to eliminate child labor or products that were a huge disappointment to both parties can reinforce similar interests. Talking about things people have in common makes them feel more connected.

### Warning others

When faced with a particularly severe product failure, consumers are more likely to generate NSWOM to warn others about the negative effects of a product or service. They have endured a negative experience and decided to share it to help other people avoid it. This is particularly relevant in food related products. Once consumers are aware of the potential harms of a product that might contain hazardous ingredients they are more likely to initiate NSWOM to warn their friends and family.

### Informing others

When faced with a bad experience, consumers will relate the experience to their network to inform them and help them in their decision-making. This information can be helpful to others as they progress in their consumer journey. Their willingness to share stems from a desire to provide their peers with the needed information to conduct their purchases, or in some case to not conduct purchases. Since NSWOM is more sensitive and controversial than positive eWOM, consumers believe it's their duty to inform others, especially if they estimate that others do not know the information yet.

## Contextual factors as a drive for NSWOM

Contextual motivations for NSWOM include all the reasons that are beyond either self-interested or socially oriented, but rather relevant to the company's actions as well as SNS use. They have gained theoretical interest in explaining NSWOM. They include, but are not limited to, firm injustice and SNS intensity (Balaji et al., 2016).

The feeling of injustice is the degree to which the failure is perceived as unfair, unequal, and unacceptable by the consumer. Studies suggest that the more severe the failure, the more effort consumers exert in voicing their discontent (Balaji & Sarkar, 2013), which results in NSWOM.

SNS intensity is the degree to which consumers make SNS part of their daily routine. The increased exposure to SNS will lead to increased attraction to the platform as well as better manipulation of its uses. Studies suggest that high Internet intensity is positively correlated with opinion leadership and opinion seeking (Sun & Zhang, 2006). It's also related to an increased desire to share information about products and services. Accordingly, SNS intensity is considered an antecedent to NSWOM (Balaji et al., 2016).

## Other factors that dictate information diffusion

Besides SNS related antecedents, other factors can aid message diffusion. Users' behavior differs across terminals. It has been exposed in a recent study that consumers have different behavior on different terminals used. They are more likely to create content or add comments to an existing post that they wish to share once they're on their computer, whereas the use of their smartphone (Zaraket, 2019) remains targeted at acts that require fewer efforts such as liking and reading posts. This limitation can dictate how and when information spreads on SNS.

Taking all these factors into consideration, marketers should be on the lookout for these elements since they are the triggers that get people to *create* NSWOM. Any negative information charged with emotional expression, extensive information about a brand's wrongdoings can spread very fast. They must do their best to avoid these situations by detecting NSWOM and interfering at different moments of truth.

## The impact of NSWOM on sender's behavior

People are motivated by diverse factors to initiate NSWOM. Once they click the "send" button, the message is out to their entire network, and even further. This message will have various impacts on their peers[3] but also on the senders themselves.

Lee and Song (2010) classify people who complain online into three groups: the complainers, the repliers, and the observers[4] (read posts, evaluate them and only take action if relevant to them).

**Effects of creating NSWOM on senders**

Despite its considerable effect, few studies have examined the impact of NSWOM on its sender.

The cognitive dissonance theory (Festinger, 1957) is a state of confusion caused by an imbalance of expectation and performance after encountering negative experience with a brand. The consumer is exposed to it when he feels the product/service did not meet his expectations, he will try to reduce this psychological tension and gain back cognitive consistency by expressing his negative experience. This state will lead the consumer to post NSWOM to reduce dissonance. This act can result in one of two consequences: self-prophecy and catharsis through venting (Kim et al., 2016). The self-prophecy approach (Sherman, 1980) suggests that the cognitive act of stating a behavioral intention will result in being committed to the said behavior. It will validate his initial position and attitude (Prislin et al., 2011). Therefore, once an individual has expressed his negative experience publicly through NSWOM, his future purchasing behavior from this company will be determined by this negative cognitive frame that he has developed by posting this negative message (Kim et al., 2016).

On the other hand, the opposite effect of posting NSWOM as a venting mechanism will reduce intense emotions. Venting strengthens the power of emotional release and reduces the intensity of the sender's emotions. In fact, voicing negative reactions to unsatisfying experiences brings a catharsis effect through venting (Berger, 2014). Studies suggest that venting about the workplace reduces retaliation intentions and increases well-being (Barclay & Skarlicki, 2009), while consumer complaining decreases consumer dissatisfaction (Nyer & Gopinath, 2005). Thus, by creating NSWOM, an individual is managing his own emotions by releasing tension.

**Notes**

1 See Chapter 4.
2 Chapter 4 will cover how receivers process this information and decide whether to share it or not.
3 Impacts will be discussed in the following chapter.
4 Discussed in Chapter 4.

# 4  ... this impacted other consumer's reactions

Consumers are confronted with all kinds of information on a daily basis. On social networking sites, these communications can be categorized into two parts: information that appears on the newsfeed without having been solicited by the consumer, over which he has little control[1] and information that the consumer voluntarily seeks to provide them with an answer to a problem. Some of this information is filtered in the consumer's mind. Hence, it is not processed, nor will it be available later on to aid with his decision-making process, while other information is not filtered and resides in the consumer's mind for future use (Guichard & Vanheems, 2004). In other words, NSWOM can be intentional and sought as well as serendipitous and not goal-oriented (Bailey, 2005).

Similar to its predecessor, traditional word of mouth, communication through electronic word of mouth on social network sites influences a multitude of factors related to the consumer's attitude towards the brand, the adoption of the information, the emotional and cognitive reaction and the behavioral intention of the consumer. These influences will be covered in this chapter, but first, it's essential to comprehend how consumers process this information.

## How receivers process NSWOM

### Processing persuasive communication

At the heart of NSWOM is just another communication. The objective of most communication is to persuade. Going back to earlier works on persuasion and rhetoric, Aristotle argued there are three main communication characteristics: ethos (how the person speaks to entice believability), pathos (the sender's emotional appeal), and logos (the sender's logical appeal) (Harrison-Walker, 2001). Ethos relates to the way the sender delivers the message to entice trust and credibility. While ethos is an important aspect, WOM sender often enriches their messages with meaningful content that has depth, intensity, and vividness (Mazzarol et al., 2007). Thus, senders would resort to a vivid and evocative language to describe their messages (pathos). The strength of delivery, which refers to the power in delivering the message (Sweeney et al., 2012) is important. It was proven that messages are more influential when they are delivered with enthusiasm (Gremler, 1994). In fact, messages that are rich in descriptions and vivid information are better retained in the receiver's memories (Herr et al., 1991). This also proves that emotion has an important role in the transmission of WOM (Soderlund & Rosengren, 2007). The logos dimension of WOM content refers to the cognitive appeal of the message. Consumers often practice rational reasoning when engaging in WOM by describing the performance, problem-solving mechanisms, and price perceptions (Sundaram et al., 1998). Receivers of these messages, in turn, form rational perceptions of the products (Allsop et al., 2007). These elements are important to understand how senders conceive their messages, but also how receivers process them.

So how does the receiving process happen?

In the communication literature, it has been noted that consumers process information in the following order: stimulus exposition, attention, understanding, acceptance, and impact (McGuire, 1968).

1. The first step in processing the information is the confrontation with the **stimulus**. Not every stimulus (or information in the context of this work) is important enough to be retained by the consumer's mind. The intensity of the stimulus has to be important enough to break through the consumer's perceptual filter thus creating a certain sensation.
2. For the information to be retained by the consumer, he must pay **attention** to it. However, consumers generally only pay attention to their current preoccupations or their immediate needs. Consequently, they have selective attention that can be tricky to break. In the advertising literature, it has been shown that such attention can be attained through the size of the ad (the bigger, the better), its positioning, its colors, its movement, and its chocking content.
3. Once the consumer retains the information, he will process it by interpreting the message through his cognitive abilities. **Understanding** the information is a cognitive process that entails confronting the stimulus with pre-existing information in the consumers' minds.

4. Understanding a piece of information does not necessarily entail accepting it. Consumers might deem the information not credible and reject it. If the information contradicts his initial beliefs about a certain brand or product he might refuse it, whereas information that does not bother his preconceived thought is more likely to be **accepted**.

5. Once information is perceived, understood, and accepted, the consumer does not automatically retain it. The credibility of the information constitutes a major element in its capacity to be stored in the consumer's mind and having an **impact** on his future behaviors.

The cognitive theories of persuasion and attitude formation have brought independent but very similar propositions. They state that the processing of information is done on two different levels. These are dual-process models such as the model of normative and informational influences based on the work of Deutsch and Gerard (1955), the ELM, or the Elaboration Likelihood Model of Petty and Cacioppo (1981; 1986) and the heuristic systematic HSM model developed by Chaiken (1980). The third method of analysis is evoked by Holbrook and Hirschman (1982), which is based on an experiential approach integrating affective dimensions.

Based on the work of McGuire (1968) and Greenwald (1968), the ELM model provides a relevant framework for understanding and analyzing the effects of persuasive communication, particularly in advertising (Petty & Cacioppo 1983). The latter was initially developed in line with theories of cognitive responses to explain contradictory research findings, particularly the affect of persuasive messages on attitude change (Petty & Cacioppo 1986). The literature provided explanations for the persuasive effects, but the divergence focused on how messages circulated to develop information. In addition, the ELM model, unlike the Yale model, puts the receiver on the same footing as the source by emphasizing the active role of the latter. According to the founders of this model, there is a continuum in the cognitive processing (elaboration) of a persuasive message. They explain that to analyze the content of a message, the cognitive effort engaged by the subject is dependent on two factors: the motivation of the individual to analyze the information and his ability to develop its content.

Depending on the attention paid to the messages, subjects will be more inclined to use one of two lanes: the *central route* or the *peripheral route*. Individuals with strong development skills and motivation will take the central route. Their choice is motivated by the critical and advanced analysis of the arguments presented in the message. The judgment of the content is based on the quality of the arguments and the result of a thorough reflection. The resulting attitude is strong, persistent, and the behavior that results, more predictable. This is confirmed by other research. A strong attitude is characterized by its stability, its proven impact on the processing of information, its resistance to change, and its behavioral orientation (Verplanken, 1991). Changes in brand perceptions occurring through the central route tend to be more enduring since they result from a deeply processed reasoning (Cialdini et al., 1981).

On the other hand, the peripheral route is a shortcut taken when the individual is not very motivated and has only a limited capacity to analyze the message. To form an attitude, the subject will favor the use of superficial clues at the expense of a thorough analysis. These include elements such as physical appearance (DeBono & Telesca, 1990) or audience reaction (Axsom et al., 1987). In this case, the judgment will be based on apparent and superficial evidence. Consequently, attitude formed through this route will be fragile, subject to temptations of counter-persuasion, and less predictable of the future behaviors of the individual.

Depending on the strength of the stimuli (the NSWOM), its recipient will determine how and if he will process the information at all. Visual content and emotionally charged messages have higher processing ability since they catch the eye of the recipient. As such, Stieglitz and Dang-Xuan (2013) found that tweets with intense emotion are retweeted faster and more often than neutral tweets.

### Factors taken into account while processing NSWOM

Three important factors must be taken into account when discussing how individuals process information generally, but more specifically NSWOM, these factors are: appraisal, attribution, and memory.

### Appraisal

Appraisal is the first act consumers will undergo when processing NSWOM. It's a mental process through which consumers will evaluate the stimuli. The recipient of NSWOM will judge the meaning of the message based on his own thoughts, feelings, and experiences. This mental evaluation will lead to particular emotions and cognitions that will serve as guidance to behavioral intentions.

*Attribution*

According to the attribution theory, individuals need to make causal analysis to understand social events and determine how to react. NSWOM recipients will process the message and make judgments about the potential causes that motivated the creation of the message, whether it's related to the company, the sender of the message, or other external circumstances. These attributions will lead the recipients to take action towards the company. They are based on (Laczniak et al., 2001):

•   Consensus, which represents the extent to which other individuals agree with the negative post.
•   Distinctiveness is the association of the message with a specific brand.
•   Consistency refers to the extent to which the sender of the message is stable over time and across situations.

NSWOM message recipients will blame the brand when all three dimensions are high in the NSWOM and the sender of the message when the dimensions are low, assuming that the issue is unique to the sender. The degree to which the receiver of the message believes the brand is responsible for the failure is the firm attribution (Zhu et al., 2013). Studies argue that this attribution is strong in the mindset of the message recipient who's only viewing the NSWOM without participating in the conversation, thus impacting his future behavioral intentions towards the company (Kim et al., 2016).

*Memory*

Most human activities rely on information inscribed in the mental system. Accordingly, memory constitutes a crucial element for understanding human behaviors (Delgadillo & Escalas, 2004). Memory processing includes two main phases: encoding information received and retrieving them when needed for thinking or decision making (Bettman, 1979).

Memory plays an important part in consumer's behavioral reactions following exposure to NSWOM. Once consumers view and process the negative communication (thoroughly or peripherally), they will store it in their minds depending on their implications with the subject of the communication and their immediate needs. What determines this retention? The content NSWOM will determine how likely it will be retained in the receiver's memory. Both the style of the message as well as its cognitive and affective intensity would enhance its retention. In fact, extensive work in psychology has demonstrated that narrative content enhances memory (Tulving & Pearlstone, 1966; Schank & Abelson, 1995). Moreover, studies on memory formation argue that people are more likely to remember important messages or emotional ones (Storbeck & Clore, 2008).

In terms of the nature of the failure and memory retention, Hansen et al. (2018) found that value-based failures don't have a strong impact on memory, especially when they're not immediately or directly relevant to the receiver. Memory fades. Events that outrage consumers today might do so in the long run which explains why many firestorms fade out over time. Nevertheless, the study also found that firestorms regarding product or service failure increase an individual's motivation to process the NSWOM, this information will not be vaguely remembered afterward, but will be deeply rooted in the consumer's memories.

## Impact of NSWOM on cognition and emotions

Once consumers undergo processing NSWOM, a sequence of interrelated emotions and cognitions will be activated in their minds. The Stimuli-Organism-Response (SOR) paradigm can be cited to elucidate this process. It specifies that the environment is a stimulus containing several signals that can impact an individual's internal evaluation, which in turn triggers responses (Arora, 1982; Houston & Rotschild, 1977). Applied to SNS, the framework stipulates that user-generated content such as bad pricing, defective products, child labor, and so on (S) would incite cognitive and emotional responses (O) in the consumer's internal that would, in turn, influence his behavioral reactions (R). In other words, once a user is exposed to a post on a social networking site that defames a product, it would immediately generate cognitive and affective message related responses (Kim & Johnson, 2016), which would, in turn, dictate his behavioral actions. These processes include feelings, physiological activities, and perceptual thinking.

Through the SOR model, consumers might encounter diverse response sequences such as a cognitive process, affective process, and a parallel process. These processes are a result of organism-generated reactions evoked when exposed to a stimulus (Bagozzi, 1983).

The cognitive process stipulates that cognitions occur before emotional responses. These cognitions include thoughts, perceptions, and beliefs formed from the processing of the stimulus (the advertisement, the word of mouth etc.). In the WOM context, this would entail that when confronted with a NSWOM communication that contains product information, the cognition is mobilized to make sense of the facts presented. Once this information is processed and understood, they would trigger an affective or emotional reaction towards the communication (Bagozzi, 1983). Using the cognitive appraisal theory, Breitsohl and Garrod (2016) found that following an unethical incident, tourists will engage in cognitive evaluations by evaluating their perceptions of the degree of severity of the incident, the image of the destination, and the attribution of blame. Consequently, emotional reactions occur (anger, disgust, and so on), which then translates into behavioral intentions.

Conversely, the affective model argues that a stimulus would induce an affective state (anger, frustration) that would, in turn, result in a cognitive reaction. In practice, consumers are exposed to a captivating positive (a great experience) or negative message (a product failure or company misconduct) and this stimulus would create emotional responses. These reactions will induce cognitive activities that include finding ways to purchase the product or considering the credibility of the message to form an opinion about the information.

At last, the parallel response argues that both cognitive and affective responses occur at the same time (Bagozzi, 1983). The emotional appeal in the stimulus is strong enough to incite a response, but not strong enough to shadow the cognitive information. When both responses are ellicited, each one of them affects response. NSWOM relates consumers experiences with a product failure or unethical behavior on behalf of the company, thus, it contains facts and triggers emotion, since negatively valanced information has been proven to be more diagnostic (i.e. provide more informational value and is adequate for decision making) than positive WOM and enables more emotional reactions (Folse et al., 2016).

*Cognitive processing of NSWOM*

Cognitive attitude is the extent to which people develop beliefs towards a target. This attitude varies in different contexts. For example, perceived usefulness was analyzed in the context of the adoption of information technology, trust was examined in the context of online shopping. Perceived credibility was also a recurrent concept in the study of online reviews. In the context of WOM, the cognitive state refers to how individuals evaluate the information they receive and make their own perceptions and judgments based on the information and cues related to the source (whether the source is known or not). Thus, perceived credibility constitutes an essential cognitive reaction and represents the extent to which individuals perceive NSWOM to be believable.

The abundance and ease of access to this source of information raise new challenges in terms of the judgment of credibility. However, the quality of the messages, their veracity, and their source is more than ever subject to consideration. Individuals are now confronted with a new challenge: how to collect reliable information from all those available on the Internet? The task is laborious, especially since the difficulty of evaluating the information is added to a large number of characteristics specific to the digital context.

In fact, the problem of the credibility of a message is not peculiar to the digital universe but it has always been at the center of people's quest for information. As for new developments induced by the Internet, Flanagin and Metzger (2008) argue that it does not concern the judgmental skills of the subjects or the cognitive mechanisms underlying them in the processing of information. Eysenbach (2008) adds that in a digital context, it's a direct relationship between the customer and the business without traditional intermediaries such as customer advisors or sellers. Individuals are now forced to self-assess the information they consult online.

Credibility has attracted the interest of many researchers whose sources sometimes go back to the oldest known writings of our civilization. Researchers agree that it represents the degree of the believability of a source or content of a message (Flanagin & Metzger, 2007). Hovland et al. (1953) defined credibility as the degree with which the receiver deems the information credible. He adds that this judgment is much of the perception of the subjects. Credibility is therefore dependent on the reliability and the expertise of the source of information as interpreted and perceived by the receiver (Ohanian, 1990).

It appears that the credibility of an online message will be jointly determined by the content and the evaluation of the elements related to its author (Cheung & Thadani, 2012; Fan et al., 2013). A multitude of works attempts to understand the influence of these two antecedents on credibility. The importance of the perceived credibility of a message and its potential in changing consumer decisions has been widely demonstrated (Gretzel et al., 2007). Since the work of Hovland (1951), the literature has consistently confirmed that a message that is perceived as credible has significant persuasive power. Through a conceptual framework that focuses on cognitive theories and theories of influence, it has since been proved that a credible source affects attitudes, purchase intentions, and consumer behavior (Chaiken, 1978; Mills & Jellison, 1967; Clow et al., 2006).

FACTORS IMPACTING CREDIBILITY

There are many antecedents for perceived message credibility. Most relevant ones include tie strength and message characteristics. Several studies on SNS have indicated that social ties have an impact on informational flow. As such, Brown and Reingen (1987) have proved that messages generated by strong ties have a higher impact on the receiver's reasoning and decision-making process than those emanating from weak ties. Contrariwise, proponents of Mark Granovetter's (1977) strength of weak tie theory have argued that weak ties have a bigger impact on information diffusion (Zhao et al., 2010). Nevertheless, people who share strong ties will spend more time talking about their consumption experiences since they are well acquainted, whereas people with weak ties spend more time together and get to know each other thus, strong ties will more likely engage in eWOM than weak ones (Zhao et al., 2012). Furthermore, Pan and Chiou (2011) found that negative eWOM trustworthiness is increased when it is generated by strong ties. Also, Kim and Rifon (2016) conducted an experiment to analyze the role of tie strength on negative eWOM. They found that higher tie strength leads to higher tweet[2] credibility.

When processing NSWOM, people will determine the credibility of the message based on the strength of its informational content. The cognitive reasoning elaborated in the message will entice persuasiveness. Similar findings in the literature demonstrate the influence of message related elements on perceived credibility such as argument quality (Cheung et al., 2009; Lee et al., 2008; Park et al., 2007). Zaraket's (2019) results confirm that eWOM receivers are more likely to be persuaded by higher informational quality and message clarity (Karmarkar & Tormala, 2010).

Many factors compose affective message characteristics for NSWOM as previously cited. Kim and Rifon's (2016) findings proved that greater levels of emotional intensity in NSWOM lead to greater perceived credibility. Linguistics, psychology, and communication experts have also argued that emotional language enhances persuasiveness (Folse et al., 2016). Studies on linguistic intensity or the extent to which a message is different than a neutral position (Bowers, 1963) and linguistic extremity or the stylings that increase the extreme position of a message (Hamilton & Stewart, 1993) have noted their influence in increasing perceived credibility of the message (Hamilton, 1998; Aune & Kikuchi, 1993).

Contrary to other social networking sites such as Twitter where the space of writing is limited to 280 characters,[3] or Instagram where the image is the core element of focus, not the text, Facebook enables users to express their negative messages with no text or visual limits. Users can freely relate the stories of their product and service failures with their peers while including as many details as they want with as much visual content to support their message. This increases the affective message characteristics possibilities, not to mention the constant updates the platform performs to make the content more visible, such as the possibility of coloring the font of the message or putting it in italics. All these platform possibilities have created more ways to increase message intensity and in turn causing higher perceived credibility of the message through strong message delivery.

*Emotional processing of NSWOM*

Before discussing emotions in consumer behavior, it is important to establish a differentiation between several affective aspects. Affect refers to the large category that includes mental processes such as emotions, moods, and attitudes (Bagozzi et al., 1999). It is a long-term state. Emotions represent the mental state that is triggered by the cognitive appraisal of events or ideas; they are intense and short term (Watson et al., 1988). In contrast, moods are more difficult to determine, nevertheless, they are intentional, longer, and have a lower intensity than emotions. Finally, attitudes are instances of affect but some scholars view them as evaluative judgments (Cohen & Areni, 1991).

Emotions are subjective states that occur as a result of feeling towards a particular target. They can vary based on time, place, and situation. They are complemented by physiological mechanisms and expressed physically through gestures and facial expressions (Bagozzi et al., 1999). They can be followed by acts that aim at confirming or coping with them depending on the nature of emotions and the individual experiencing them. Emotions are usually described through their valence (positive or negative) and their nature (joy, anger etc.). Damasio (2011) affirms that emotions are actions or movements that are public and visible to others as they appear on their faces, in the voice, and through specific behaviors.

What kind of emotions do NSWOM receivers experience when they're exposed to these messages? They can range from apathy to negative emotions.

According to Watson et al. (1988), negative affect is the extent to which individuals experience anger, frustration, and irritation. Most research that focused on negative emotion as a result of consumption experiences agrees on these negative emotions. In fact, Reynolds et al.

(2006) found that following unsatisfying shopping experiences, consumers will experience negative feelings that include irritation, frustration, and anger. Moon et al. (2016) finding also suggested that anger is directly related to negative eWOM. Other scholars found that regret and disappointment had a significant effect on eWOM (Zeelenberg & Peiters, 2004).

There has been a lot of work relative to negative emotion especially as a reaction to a service failure. Breitsohl and Garrod (2016) use Izard's (1977) hostility triad of emotions: namely anger, contempt, and disgust, which has recently been shown to be experienced by consumers in the context of an unethical incident (Grappi, Romani, & Bagozzi, 2013). Kahr et al. (2016) resort to aggressive consumer behavior theories to explain negative emotions: frustration, anger, outrage, and hatred. Park (2016) measured negative emotions by asking participants to report the extent to which they experienced negative emotions while browsing online news websites. The following emotions were used: overwhelmed, frustrated, confused, discouraged, impatient, disoriented, bored, and irritated. Verhagen et al. (2013) used emotions that represent basic reactions that were applied to different consumption settings, including the following emotions: anger, frustration, irritation, unfulfilled, and discontentment.

Negative emotions are felt by recipients who process NSWOM without having lived the negative experience first-hand due to emotional contagion. Zaraket (2019) found that negative emotions transpire through NSWOM. The closer the tie between the sender and the receiver, the stronger the negative emotions felt by the receiver.

Emotional contagion has been proven to appear through nonverbal communication. Some authors even emphasized that these nonverbal cues are necessary for contagion (Ekman, 1992). Nevertheless, recent studies have begun to analyze these phenomena through computer-mediated systems (Guillory et al., 2011). Since human interactions have moved online, more specifically on social networking sites, more authors have taken interest in analysis in the transposition of emotional contagion onto the online context (Kramer, 2012). The author studies whether and how emotional contagion happens on social networking sites. He found that when users post happy emotions about an event that occurred their friends will automatically generate positive emotions based on the event itself. Thus, the mere exposure to the message written in a certain style on Facebook (even if it's not directly addressed to a particular friend), will lead to emotional mimicry. In other words, reading other people's negative eWOM would lead to the same negative emotions as the ones felt by the senders of the message through emotional contagion. Negative emotions will serve as a basis for making judgments for future behaviors. According to the affect as information theory, the emotional state of individuals has an effect on their assessment of the possible decisions to make (Zadra & Clore, 2011). This theory has been used to analyze the role of emotions in eWOM processing (Soderlund & Rosengren, 2007). It is often used when making quick heuristic judgments (Forgas, 1995). Previous work has proved that affect can trigger judgmental reactions that are faster in nature and more consistent among people (Shih et al., 2013). When faced with a stimulus, consumers resort to an internal processing mechanism in which they ask themselves how the target object makes them feel and act accordingly. Individuals would infer the strength of their responses based on the intensity and valence of their affect (Argyriou & Melewar, 2011) Thus, if the stimulus makes them feel bad, they will feel bad towards the target object. In a qualitative study, Salerno et al. (2017) found that emotions experienced by theater subscribers through the show, the social experience, and the peripheral services have a significant effect on their sustainable loyalty behavior.

FACTORS IMPACTING EMOTIONS

Not only does the emotional appeal of NSWOM impact its perceived credibility, but it also positively influences negative emotions felt by the receiver. The higher the intensity of the NSWOM, the higher the transfer of negative emotions to the receiver (Zaraket, 2019). Hardly any research has tackled the effects of reading negative eWOM on consumer emotions, even less addressed the role of affective message characteristics on the receiver's emotions. However, Guillory et al. (2011) have conducted a study in which they found that interpersonal emotions were shared among group members through linguistic cues.

Given the fact that SNS gather people of different relationships such as acquaintances, close friends, colleagues, or even family members, it can be said that the emotional effect of reading a NSWOM does not depend solely on the composition of the message, but also on the relationship with the sender. The stronger the bond between the sender and the receiver of the NSWOM, the stronger the receiver will generate negative emotions towards the brand in question as a result of emotional contagion.

*The reaction towards the message: adoption of the message*

Cognitive and emotional elaboration will lead to a response on behalf of the recipient of NSWOM regarding the content of the message: its adoption. It consists of deciding whether to accept or reject the NSWOM. NSWOM can have important consequences for harming companies. However, if consumers do not accept the message, nothing will change (Chang & Wu, 2014). Adoption of the communication is defined as the process by which individuals voluntarily commit to using information (Cheung et al., 2009, Sussman & Siegal, 2003). According to Lee and Koo (2012), this is the degree of acceptance of the message by the reader after evaluating its content. Moreover, Sussman and Siegal (2003) add that adoption is a construct that is intimately linked to the usefulness of the information contained in the notice, which reflects the informational influence of the latter. This implies that a consumer who adopts an opinion must accept the recommendations of the consumer, which is essentially a result of an action.

Adoption of the message is the measure of persuasiveness and a consequence of eWOM according to literature (Cheung et al., 2012; Cheung et al., 2009). The importance of NSWOM resides in the fact that it is taken into consideration in the recipients' purchase decision making (Gershoff et al., 2003). Also, the most important phase in information persuasion is the one where the recipient judges the credibility of the information. This is when the receiver adopts the information (Wathen & Burkell, 2002). If recipients decide to adopt negative eWOM, they will have knowledge of the product, avoid wrong purchasing choices, and change their prior feelings about the brand (Chang & Wu, 2014).

High arousal emotions such as anger are more likely to enhance information acceptance and diffusion than low arousal emotions (Breitsohl & Garrod, 2016). As stated, SNS users are likely to experience negative emotions as a result of being exposed to NSWOM emanating from members of their network through emotional contagion. The greater these negative emotions the higher the adoption of the negative message.

*Reactions towards the brand: behavioral impacts*

The next step in the information process is the response of the recipient of the NSWOM. What are the possible options? Logically, they include reacting to the communication or ignoring it. Consumers who ignore the message are less likely to take any action until they recognize that there is an issue relevant to them. Concerning the reactions they can be proactive or less reactive. The intensity of the reaction depends on message characteristics (cognitive and emotional), tie strength, receiver characteristics, and other factors.

Bagozzi (1986) defines response as the outcome or final action toward or reaction of consumers, including psychological reactions such as attitudes and/or behavioral reactions. Wundt (1905) argued that behaviors due to mood and environment evaluation can be classified as approach or avoidance.

Breitsohl et al. (2016) resort to the cognitive appraisal theory to qualify these behaviors as coping strategies in which consumers engage when dealing with stressful situations. These include being exposed to unethical incidents. The authors found that these avoidance behaviors are directly influenced from consumer's hostile emotions. Coping refers to the act of dealing with stressful situations. Coping is a two dimensional model: the most reliable measurement in the literature distinguishes between coping that is focused inwardly (focused on emotions) or focused outwardly (focused on the problem) (Chebat et al., 2005). Thus, when experiencing negative emotions, individuals might concentrate on managing their emotions by distancing themselves from the incident. This avoidance grants them emotional relief (Folkman et al., 1986). These coping strategies occur in a situation of crisis. Otherwise, the individual might analyze the problem outwardly and decide to employ negative WOM as a coping mechanism. This mechanism is harmful since it is the most credible and highly transmittable. Very few studies have attempted to analyze avoidance behavior (as opposed to analyzing approach behavior). One study has focused on fear as a coping strategy resulting from emotions and avoidance (Jin, 2009).

Drawing on psychology and marketing literature, it was found that following a negative incident, individuals experience different behavioral responses that include intentions to punish (Sweetin et al., 2013), requesting additional information (Lyon & Cameron, 2004), boycotting (Sen et al., 2001), spreading negative WOM (Liu et al., 2011), and protesting (Grappi et al., 2013).

*Brand attitude and brand avoidance*

While it's logical to assume that exposure to NSWOM can lead to negative attitudes towards the brand, some studies have shown the contrary. Besides the harmful effects, NSWOM can actually be good for the brand. It was argued that committed consumers will defend the brand. Hoffman and Muller (2009) showed that the prior existence of positive brand image will buffer the negative incident, which will reduce the impact of the NSWOM and boycott campaigns. Likewise, Wilson et al. (2017) proved that negative WOM can be positive for consumers connected to the brand. Nevertheless, Khtiri and Michel (2017) found that consumers who are *not* attached to the brand will also defend it in times of crises.

Anti-consumption is of particular interest to us in relation to consumer's avoidance behavior notably brand avoidance. The latter is the *active* act of rejecting a brand; it doesn't include situations where consumers can't make their purchases due to availability, affordability, and accessibility (Lee et al., 2009). It includes behaviors made through an active choice such as abandonment (no longer purchasing a brand that was previously purchased), avoidance (keeping away or turning away from a brand), and aversion (moving away from a brand) (Hogg et al., 1998). It should be noted that brand avoidance does not exclusively include distinct incidents that formed negative attitude towards the brand and caused it rejection, but also include past events such as the company's ethical behavior over time (Strandvik et al., 2013). Accordingly, brand avoidance is the consumer's conscious act of rejecting a brand (as a result of an incident formed recently or an attitude formed over time) while having all the means to access, purchases, and get it (Hogg, 1998; Lee et al., 2009). Anti-consumption categorizations (that also apply to brand avoidance) are numerous in the literature. The most known classification is that of Kozinet et al., (2010) in which he distinguishes between avoidance based on moral concerns and avoidance based on personal concerns.

Besides the anti-consumption act of brand avoidance, consumers can adopt more active negative behaviors. Kahr et al. (2016) distinguish three types of negative consumer behavior: customer retaliation, negative word of mouth, and consumer brand sabotage (and consumer boycotts). Whereas the former aims at harming the brand as a main objective, customer retaliation and negative word of mouth only harm the brand as a means to obtain different objectives. This instrumental aggression (customer retaliation and negative word of mouth) occurs much more than consumer brand sabotage.

Once a negative eWOM is processed on SNS, how likely is it that it will be shared?

## eWOM and WOM behaviors

Positive eWOM is easier to show on Facebook since the social network was conceived in a way to encourage positive relationships with brands to promote advertising on the platform. Consequently, consumers have many possibilities to show their support of a brand: they can follow their page, like their content, invite friends to like the page, and so on. However, the negative behaviors consumers feel are not easily expressed as they are not facilitated by the platform. Facebook was even late in introducing "reaction buttons" in addition to the "like" button, which appears on posts and signal user's reactions towards the message with two buttons signaling negative emotions (they include: like, love, laugh, amazed, sad, and angry). Besides these buttons, users have formed groups and created anti-brand pages to show their disapproval of bad company behaviors. In addition, SNS users have resorted to other negative behaviors: complaining about products or brands through WOM and negative eWOM. The first is restricted to friends and family as it appears face-to-face, while the second is addressed at a wider audience since it takes place online.

It was found that negative emotions have a significant effect on WOM and eWOM retransmission. Consistent with similar theories that state that consumer's affective is related to WOM intentions (Ha & Im, 2012; Ladhari, 2007). The higher the negative emotions felt as a result of negative eWOM exposure, the higher the receiver's sharing intention. Several things motivate this. It can be assumed that people who generate negative eWOM on their feeds will likely share negative eWOM for the same reasons such as the desire to warn one's network about the potential pitfalls of the brand, the desire to appear knowledgeable in front of one's network, to inform them, but also to cause harm to the brand, and get an answer from the brand. Several authors proved that anger will result in WOM transmission (Coombs & Holladay, 2007; McDonald et al., 2010; Lindenmeier et al., 2012; Utz et al., 2013).

Social networking sites such as Facebook have made it easier to share WOM through the availability of "share" buttons (Aghakhani et al., 2016). When retransmitting NSWOM, SNS users want to be as persuasive as the sender of the message, some users tend to customize the message being retransmitted by writing a personal message to appeal to their network. The particularity of Facebook resides in the fact that it provides a lot of space for users to add any message they'd like to support their views. Twitter on the other hand offers faster information diffusion through the specificities of its system that connect many nodes rapidly; nevertheless, its textual content is limited. The use of hashtags on Instagram also favors the rapid diffusion of negative eWOM.

While social networking sites have made it easier to share content online, eWOM transmission is not a given. SNS users are concerned about their virtual image and the way they are perceived by their peers, thus, they will exert extra effort in choosing what they share. Previous research has argued that consumers choose how to share WOM based on the extent to which it provides self-enhancement (Berger & Iyengar, 2013).

*Non purchasing behaviors*

NSWOM can have a significant effect on other consumers shaping their purchasing behavior ergo impacting brands. These effects can range from not purchasing the product to actively seeking brand sabotage (Kahr et al., 2016).

Negative emotions (especially those of high arousal), are an essential part of anti-consumption frameworks (Lai & Aritejo, 2010). Literature on consumer boycott has analyzed the role of emotions in boycott behaviors and found that emotions are a predictor of boycotts (Farah & Newman, 2010; Hoffman & Muller, 2009). In other words, strong negative emotions towards the brand will influence consumer decisions to actively stop purchasing the brand as a way to harm the brand. According to the literature, there is a relationship between emotional responses arising within the consumer's internal state and their purchasing decisions and intentions. Hostile emotions arising from the experience of an unethical incident have led to different coping mechanisms, including avoidance behavior and WOM transmission (Breitsohl et al., 2016). Thus, experiencing negative emotions as a result of a negative incident will lead to an avoidance of the target. This avoidance behavior refers to future purchasing decisions.

A purchase intention is the willingness to purchase the product in the future. Non-purchase or brand avoidance refers to the willingness to delete the product from the consumer's consideration set. Following negative information about a product, consumers are faced with the decision to believe it or not. Once credibility is established, non-purchase behaviors are more likely to occur.

Nevertheless, avoidance behavior doesn't automatically occur. Zaraket (2019) found that strong negative emotions resulting from exposure to NSWOM do not influence non-purchase behaviors. It could be that the emotions felt by the receiver are not a result of his own personal experience, but that of a member of his online network, thus, they do not constitute a strong enough motivation to make such a purchasing decision. The emotions felt by the receiver are contagion emotions that transferred from the sender; if the emotions were a direct result of the negative encounter with the brand they would have more likely influenced brand avoidance. Another reason that can explain this result is the occurrence of the event and its importance. If the receiver believes that the incident is a one-time thing, he will be upset with his

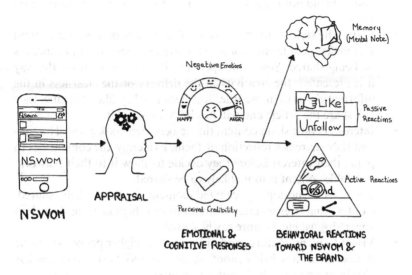

*Figure 4.1* Processing NSWOM
Courtesy of Nayla Idriss

friend for experiencing such an incident but he would not rely on these
negative emotions to make purchasing decisions and avoiding the brand.
A review of the processing of NSWOM is presented in
Figure 4.1 above.

## How does this translate for marketers? What makes a NSWOM shareable?

Beyond the reasons why message senders create NSWOM or why
recipients share this content, how can this information provide value
to marketers?

This information provides insights on what makes negative content
"shareable." Practitioners should be on the lookout and detect any kind
of NSWOM that present these elements. It can be summarized in the
following acronym: VISIE, which stands for:

• **Information.** People will share what they find valuable for them
  and their networks, such as informational content that educates
  and brings new material. People consumers are reluctant to post
  NSWOM if they deem that their peers already know the information

and it would not make any difference if they share the information or not.

- **Style**. The style of the message is of high importance. Fun content that makes people laugh or satire or even memes have more chances of being shared. Sometimes people will share content for the way it is presented, the creativity in the delivery or the clearness in the information or even the title. Just because they liked the title, they will share the article and will not bother to read it.
- **Interest**. People share content that makes them look good. The content they share is a reflection of them. Evidently, the content has to pique their interest before they decide to show it to their network. Relatable content is more likely to be shared.
- **Emotions**. Emotionally charged content is more likely shared. Content that triggers intense emotions or is high in arousal, such as anger, disgust etc. is more easily shared.
- **Visual Content**. Pictures and videos have a higher propensity to be shared since they bring proof about the NSWOM. Vividness has also been proven to be important in processing information.

## Notes

1  Social networking sites such as Facebook are constantly updating their features. During the time of this book, Facebook had made it possible to customize one's Newsfeed by selecting the kind of information they wish to receive and the kind of information they wish to avoid.
2  A tweet is a message on the social networking site Twitter.
3  The word count has been moved to 280 characters in 2018. It used to be 140 characters.

# 5 So how can you deal with NSWOM?

Studies have shown that a proper reaction to NSWOM crisis can have a positive impact on advocacy, trust, and customer satisfaction and help regain loyalty (Lee & Song, 2010). They can also make way for a change in the company's strategies. The JetBlue crisis has resulted in the creation of the Customer Bill of Rights, whereas Domino's viral video showing employees doing disgusting things with the pizza caused the brand to shift tactics. Their turnaround eventually led to $12b in enterprise value (Aaron Allen & Associates, 2018).

Managing these online platforms well gives marketers an excellent opportunity to turn a negative comment into an engagement opportunity. In fact, the webcare literature shows that actively looking for NSWOM and offering an adequate remedy can turn a negative situation into a positive one (Lee & Song, 2010; Van Noort & Willemsen, 2011). So how should brand managers deal with SNS?

## Before the crisis/NSWOM: monitoring social network sites

It takes years to build a brand reputation up to certain expectations, to gain consumer trust, and to achieve a desired space in the consumers' minds. But it takes a moment to destroy it. Having the information at the tips of their fingers and with a simple click of a button (Kahr et al., 2016), consumers can become hostile and attack brands (Labrecque et al., 2013), thus causing them irreparable damage.

### *Anticipating value-based failures...*

There's an old French saying: *Mieux vaut prévenir que guérir.*[1] It's always best to anticipate problems, to be proactive rather than reactive. The ideal way to do that is by actively looking for NSWOM that can be significantly problematic and can snowball into a firestorm such as ethical, social or communication mishaps.

Needless to say, before worrying about NSWOM, a brand must have established their image. Brands must always act according to their desired perceived image. Once their identity is set, every action they take publicly should take into account this factor. This mindset helps build stronger, more credible brands. The consistency will entice brand commitment and trust, which will help defend the brand if it ever encounters a crisis.

Once brands highlight their company values, consumers will hold them accountable for it. In the wake of the Black Lives Matter Movement, it's not enough to post a blackout picture,[2] people want to hear about the concrete actions taken by brands to support the movement. Once a brand has posted a blackout picture, it's under scrutiny as its actions are expected to express this support. Based on a scrupulous observation of numerous accounts of brands (notably in the beauty industry), a serious demand of accountability from consumers can be observed. A movement even emerged asking major companies to pull up and reveal their staff diversity (#PullUpForChange). They're calling out brands to prove they enforce inclusive policies, some brands have anticipated accountability and immediately worked on shifting their strategies, such as Frank Body, by amending their diversity policies, matching donations of its team to fight racial injustice and altering their marketing efforts to be more diverse. Anticipation and responsiveness are crucial in such cases.

### ... and product/service based failures

Most product and service failures are raised through consumers' complaints. Previously, complaining consisted of two-way communication between a dissatisfied customer and the company. Today, consumers are voicing their complaints with other consumers on SNS turning the two-way communication into a triadic communication involving third parties that witness the complainant's message and reactions towards the brand as well as their response (Van Noort et al., 2015). When a SNS user shares a dissatisfying experience with a brand on these platforms, he's not just engaging in NSWOM, but also a compliant behavior. His message is addressed to both the company of the negative experience as well as other (potential) consumers (Van Noort et al., 2015). Companies have enforced webcare strategies to answer these complaints.

Therefore, it's also crucial to be responsive to consumer complaints. Studies showed that consumers will resort to SNS because it's easier to get a response from the company, especially when you mention them. Moreover, when consumers are frustrated with unresponsive customer support, a complaint on social media seems like the best strategy to catch their attention (Zaraket, 2019). Therefore, brands must make it very easy for consumers to complain to them directly so they won't take their discontent online. Any action taken into that direction is a good one, whether it's hiring more people to handle customer complaints or automating the process of receiving customer complaints.

A plan should be elaborated to address *both* the brand's offensive and defensive strategies. It's advisable not to wait to be taken by an online crisis to react and utilize defensive actions, but rather encourage an offensive attitude encouraging positive eWOM and foster a sense of trust among consumers to avoid these situations in the first place at best, and to detect the bud of the crisis at worst.

*Tracking conversations about the brand*

The first step in countering NSWOM is to beat it before it reaches the brand, *find NSWOM before it finds you.* SNS allows every user to speak their minds and express themselves about their consumption, it's already been established that this presents a great opportunity for brands to conduct market studies and listen to how the consumers want to conceive new products (co-creation), it's equally beneficial for practitioners to listen in on consumers' conversations to track their brand reputation and identify potential "bottlenecks" that can escalate if not addressed properly.

In this phase, brands must listen to whatever is being said about them, the good and the bad. The sphere of this analysis should not be limited to complaints directly addressed to the brand or eWOM where senders actually mention the brand (by using the "@" followed by the brand name). A thorough tracking would involve *listening* to all conversations talking about the brand. Complaints can happen any time but so can crisis. Consumers will hold on to every word. Many times brands won't even see it coming. They would think they've crafted the perfect communication strategy, only to see it go sideways. Sometimes it can just take one word, one word that can be interpreted differently can cause serious damage. During the 2017 Boston Marathon, Adidas sent an email to the participants with the heading "Congrats, you survived the Boston Marathon!" While this sentence can seem humorous in any other context, it was not in this case; participants were outraged and considered the message to be insensitive since four years earlier a terrorist attack occurred during the same marathon taking the lives of three people. Thankfully, the brand was reactive by retracting the message, issuing an apology the same day, thus, avoiding a potential crisis.

Given the large volume of consumer-generated content on SNS, it has become quite difficult for marketing professionals to identify and analyze eWOM about their products and services. Both academic and professional studies encourage the use of sentiment analysis to help identify this eWOM to take appropriate measures since it measures consumer sentiment in real-time. Sentiment analysis is a computer-based analysis of a written text that aims to detect the attitudes and opinions of its authors about specific topics. Through emotional artificial intelligence, it provides an overview of the overall valence (positive or negative) and intensity (strong or weak) of the sentiments conveyed in the text (Stieglitz & Dang-Xuan, 2013). Most sentiment analysis available in the market is based on automated language processing models (SentiStrength, SentiGem, MeaningCloud, and so on). They account for semantics as well as users' opinion intensifiers such as using capital letters, exclamation marks, profanities, and emoticons.[3]

Sentiment analysis is believed to be a good tool for detecting NSWOM. It has been used in boycott research (Makarem & Jae, 2016). However, these tools may not be enough. Vermeer et al. (2019) argue the way these tools are used is not ideal since they follow the postulate according to which it's only worthwhile to respond to NSWOM, moreover, they are unable to deduce meaning from textual statements. In fact, some researchers argue that automated sentiment analysis tools are unable to detect sarcasm or go over text that uses slang and problematic punctuation (Feldman, 2013). Instead, Makarem and Jae (2016) resort to human sentiment analysis executed by coders to address these limitations.

Drasch et al. (2015) created an Online Firestorm Detector that's specifically targeted at alerting companies of potential negative escalations of NSWOM by inciting their early adoption. It can reliably detect the emergence of online firestorms right after the first piece of related negative communication has been generated. This IS artifact works in three steps: it monitors social media and collects eWOM, conducts sentiment analysis, and finally, detects the emergence of online firestorms. One of the particularities of this detector lies in the fact that it considers both positive and negative eWOM, which ultimately leads to a lower number of false alarms than other tools that rely solely on NSWOM.

On the other hand, Vermeer et al. (2019) argue that there's a need to resort to tools that are more reliable and accurate than sentiment analysis to determine SWOM that are in immediate need of a response. They claim sentiment analysis is unable to identify content factors of eWOM, such as argument diversity and review subjectivity. Instead, they believe supervised machine learning methods that focus on context and relevance of content are a better option to identify relevant SWOM for brands. Relevant eWOM includes all statements concerning the product, the service, or the entire brand. Supervised machine learning algorithms would learn from the coder's decision as to determine whether the eWOM is worth a response or not, which solves the classification problem for large eWOM messages. Moreover, this tool was able to go beyond detecting dissatisfaction; it also determined positive and neutral eWOM that requires a response, which sentiment analysis usually does not address even though they constitute an important factor worth addressing. This technique is widely being used in consumer research (Ordenes et al., 2018; Homburg et al., 2015; Okazaki et al., 2015).

Whatever the tools, the important part for marketers is to listen to what SNS users are saying about the brand, the good and the bad, gather the data and analyze it to determine which communications need to be addressed.

### Determining NSWOM to be addressed

Once the tracking phase is complete, how should brands decide which messages to address?

The first decision to make is whether to reply at all. Some messages should be ignored while others can incur significant damages if not addressed, such as the Dave Carroll example. When people consider brand responses as intrusive or unsolicited it may be harmful to brand perceptions (Noort et al., 2014).

On the other hand, the act of remaining silent constitutes a response strategy (no-response strategy) in itself. It has consequences on brand perceptions that must be taken into account. Some studies found that response strategies might have negative impacts on purchase intentions and brand performance (Xie et al., 2014). It can also give the impression that the brand is not being honest and authentic. However, it is not always a negative effect. In fact, this strategy can minimize company blame and is accepted by individuals who already have strong feelings for the company (Smith, 2013). A no-response strategy would enable NSWOM about the brand to remain unchallenged, which can result in damaging the brand's image (Lee & Song, 2010). Compared to a response strategy, a no-response strategy provides less trust and consumer concern inferences (Sparks et al., 2016).

As previously discussed, the main characteristics that make a NSWOM shareable are: visual, informative, interesting, high in emotions content, and captivating style. These elements should be taken into consideration when analyzing which communications to address. Professionals and researchers agree on the importance of providing a timely response, especially in a critical situation that demands immediate action. In deciding how to prioritize NSWOM that needs a faster reply, detecting the ones that would cause the most damage is crucial. Early warning indicators must be established to be able to provide the appropriate measures (Hansen et al., 2018).

Choosing *when* to respond and *who* to react to have a significant impact on the way a crisis will evolve. Ott and Theunissen (2015) analyzed three brand responses to a crisis and found that responding directly and automatically to all individuals can make a crisis worse, while refraining from replying at all can lead to lesser emotional attacks. A third option favors a more strategic and selective approach whereby the targeted company would only communicate with customers directly impacted by the brand failure while ignoring other angry users. This method enabled the resolution of the problem and prevented it from escalating.

Nevertheless, PSWOM and neutral eWOM on SNS should also be addressed alongside NSWOM to show responsiveness and encourage positive reactions amidst a crisis. Even at times free of crisis, these messages should be addressed to build lasting relationships with consumers and convey trust and credibility.

Most marketing professionals have established a company blueprint that explains the measures to follow when dealing with NSWOM. Several features of these blueprints have been defined, such as having response libraries to stock a pre-defined template to answer all recurrent problems or queries, or escalation plans to determine which person in the company to solicit for feedback in case of aggravation of the problem. Evidently, one size does not fit all. Each company should create its own blueprint after analyzing NSWOM. Among the topics that should be covered to train employees on how to react to NSWOM:

- Identifying which NSWOM needs an immediate response (categorizing NSWOM by priority levels).
- Determining if NSWOM should be handled in private or in public.

- Determining how different failures (i.e. value-based failure and product/service-based) should be handled.
- Establishing the tone to be used in the response.
- Determining which response strategy to adopt for different cases.

Surely, these blueprints can't cover any potential NSWOM that can arise, but they should cover main topics based on the ones the company has previously dealt with.

## During the crisis/NSWOM: response strategies

When brands adopt a response strategy, it grants them the opportunity to react promptly and can convert dissatisfied consumers into loyal ones, all the while showing transparency and authenticity by telling the brand's side of the story.

### Choosing a response strategy: accommodative or defensive?

If brands do decide to respond, the response can be reactive or proactive (Van Noort & Willemsen, 2011). The latter is when brands find NSWOM and respond to it without being solicited, whereas the former is when brands respond to NSWOM that was directly addressed to them. This response or the act of engaging with online communities, finding complaints, and addressing them is called: webcare. Webcare is similar to customer service only it takes place on SNS.

While webcare strategies are usually used to answer consumer complaints (most cases for product failures), different brand efforts should be enforced to address more serious complaints and online firestorms. Nevertheless, both kinds of responses can be categorized into three groups: no response, accommodative response, and defensive response. The first kind of response, the no-response strategy, was tackled earlier. Before delving into the benefits of response strategies, it's relevant to explore these response strategies and how they manifest in both webcare (NSWOM) and crisis response (brand crisis).

Accommodative responses include any kind of apology, compensation, and/or corrective measures. Many combinations can be made such as offering an apology alone, an apology and an explanation, an apology and compensation, an apology, an explanation and a compensation.

Apologies can be seen as a basic response. An apology is an admission of responsibility for negative events while showing remorse. Companies have resorted to apologies to convey a positive impression and attenuate the severity of failures. Studies have shown that apologies are an effective tool to regain consumer trust. However, if consumers doubt the sincerity of the apology, it can backfire. Recently, a skincare company has received such backlash. An influencer had been promoting Naturium's products since February. In June, she finally announced that she actually owns the brand. SNS users were not happy about it and did not hesitate to show their outrage, which led her to issue a public apology claiming she was not made an official co-founder yet. The apology did not resonate well with the consumers who found her tone to be condescending and believed she was only sorry she got caught since her claims of not knowing whether she'd be an official founder were hard to believe. The public was not convinced by this apology and many consumers voiced their intentions to report this act to the Federal Trade Commission as it violates the FTC guidelines. As a webcare strategy, an apology alone has become less effective.

Another measure brands take in negative situations is providing an explanation for the failure. These explanations help consumers understand the reasons behind the negative situation that might not be clear to them. They can be classified as internal or external explanations: the latter shift the blame onto someone else while the former is an admission of guilt for the problem. Combining apology and explanation has different effects. Some researchers argue that apologies and external explanations can lead to negative reactions potentially leading to mistrust (Kim et al., 2006). When faced with a crisis, a combination of apology and internal explanation can be effective. KFC mastered this strategy by combining these elements with humor when they ran out of chicken after having switched distributors. Consumers took their anger to social media so the company responded with an ad that rearranged their logo to "FCK" and a headline "We're Sorry." The ad also explained the reasons for the problem while promising it would not happen again.

Other strategies can also be classified under the accommodative response, such as the mortification strategy and the corrective strategy. The mortification strategy is when a company apologizes for the wrongdoing and asks for forgiveness, this measure can have a positive impact on the brand image since people tend to look favorably at repents (Benoit, 1997). In 2010, O.B. tampons went off the shelves due to supply issues, consumers were angry. O.B.'s parent company Johnson & Johnson listened to its consumers and to show remorse, they sent an email to over 70 000 women in their database containing an apology song customized with their names to show how sorry they were. Customers welcomed this move and shared the videos they received on social media, which turned a potential firestorm into a successful social media strategy.

The corrective action strategy is taken by brands which feel responsible for an offensive act they've caused. They promise to fix the damage or take the necessary actions to prevent it from reoccurring (Len-Ríos & Benoit, 2004). The most famous corrective action strategy is probably that of Tylenol's recall. In 1982, Tylenol issued a nationwide recall of its products after seven people died as a result of taking Tylenol pills, which were laced with a poison. The company suffered a huge financial hit: an estimated loss of $100 000 million. However, it was the first time a brand recalled its products; the company took the appropriate corrective measures. As a result, Tylenol provided new safety elements to the Tylenol bottle: cotton wad, foil seal, childproof cap, and plastic strip. The Tylenol crisis became a crisis management example.

Each one of the accommodative strategies has a different influence on consumers' brand attitude and their willingness to spread positive eWOM (Dens et al., 2015). It's important for marketing professionals to keep in mind that brands will not only be judged on what caused the occurrence of the mistake, but also (and perhaps even more) on how they responded to it. This idea has been studied extensively in the literature.

Defensive response strategies rely on shifting the blame onto others. The company will claim that they are not responsible for the failure, arguing that it was the fault of a third party (Lee & Cranage, 2014). This action might be relevant when it's hard to identify the source of the problem. However, research found that this strategy might result in negative brand perceptions (Lee, 2005). Lee and Song (2010) argue that this strategy generates less favorable brand evaluation than the accommodative response. Consumers exposed to defensive strategy are more likely to believe the company's at fault. Similarly, Weitzel (2019) found that defensive strategies are likely to trigger negative emotions among constructive complainers, which will consequently lead to NWOM generation.

Since the responses have been overly studied as opposed to characteristics, it's time to focus less on response strategies and more on effective webcare characteristics that would eliminate the negative effects of NSWOM. In other words, explore why webcare strategies are a good fit for brands to counter NSWOM.

Studies have shown that webcare is beneficial for brands and provides positive results. It impacts consumer forgiveness (Ghogh, 2017). It can incite a positive perception of the brand, not only for the complainants but also for the viewers of the NSWOM (Willemsen et al., 2013).

A study found that while offering an apology didn't have a big effect on posters (Kim et al., 2016), it had a significant effect on viewers. It increased their positive behavioral intentions. Moreover, webcare strategies convey concern for consumers (Bhandari & Rodgers, 2018), which would help brands counterbalance the negative effects of NSWOM and prevent it from escalating (Van Noort et al., 2014). Weitzl et al. (2018) found that webcare has a positive impact on failure attributions depending on prior experience with the brand and other consumers' online reviews. If consumers have had several issues with brands before, the variety of webcare will not influence them greatly. However, consumers who have experienced fewer failures with the brand will be more responsive to different kinds of webcare.

Many variables also play an important part in influencing consumers' reactions to webcare responses. Sparks et al. (2016) measured the impacts of four of them: the source of response, the voice of responder, speed of response, and action frame. First, the source of the response or the position of the person responding to the NSWOM; contrary to previous studies, this one did not highlight a positive relationship between high ranking personal responding to NSWOM and increased trust and consumer care inferences. The voice of the responder is the style of communication adopted by the responder (professional vs conversational human). Conversational human voice generates more trust and leads consumers to think that the brand genuinely cares. The speed of response is an indicator of efficiency; it's the time it takes a brand to respond to the NSWOM. It was found that a one-day lag between the complaint and the reply provides stronger trust and consumer concern inferences than a 30-day lag. The action frame represents whether the company has provided a corrective measure already or it will be taken in the future. The study found no link between the action frame and consumer inferences.

Response strategies can impact viewers not only posters, therefore it is advised that responses are tailored accordingly. Customized responses for viewers and posters are encouraged (Kim et al., 2016). Transparency and information for viewers is provided and the posters are encouraged to take part in the conversation and generate positive WOM.

## After the crisis/NSWOM: measure and monitor results

### Follow back, measure and keep track

Throughout the negative incident, brands should use metrics to analyze the outrage (Hansen et al., 2018). Measuring and analyzing the effects of the crisis will provide valuable insights to avoid its repetition in the future. Once the situation cools down, it should not be believed that the storm has passed. Marketers must follow up with complainants in the case of a service/product failure and check the overall reaction of people in the case of a value-based failure and keep track of the strategies that were effective and those that were not.

## *Monitoring online and offline communications and channels*

In a highly digitalized world, consumers are constantly moving between virtual and physical channels before making a final purchase (Vanheems, 2010). Many scholars have attempted to understand this cross channel to finding new ways to interact with consumers on different channels (Badot & Navarre, 2002; Heitz-Spahn, 2013; Collin-Lachaud & Vanheems, 2016).

Similarly, studies have found that consumers are active and they do not limit their search to one channel of choice. On one hand, SNS users are exploring different digital channels and on the other hand, brands are addressing their message through an array of digital channels to be able to interact with them. Once exposed to a NSWOM, consumers have different channels they might check for information (both online and offline): the Facebook page of the brand in question, the official website of the brand, search engines, the physical store of the brand, retailers, etc. In the case of a negative buzz, users will check the company's page and website to see its reaction. Moreover, consumer responses take place both online and offline. Consumers can hurt the brand by posting online as well as talking about it to their friends and families offline. Marketers can measure the effects of the first one through specialized tools; however, the effect of WOM is harder to measure, but should not be neglected. Marketing professionals must, therefore, monitor all their channels of communication as well as their points of sale to make sure their communications are up to date and consistent with their communication strategies.

When a value-based failure occurs, marketers are urged to prepare strategies to cope accordingly because consumers will have a cross channel behavior. They must have a crisis management strategy that encloses their different channels.

A review of the steps in dealing with NSWOM and brand crisis is presented in Figure 5.1 below.

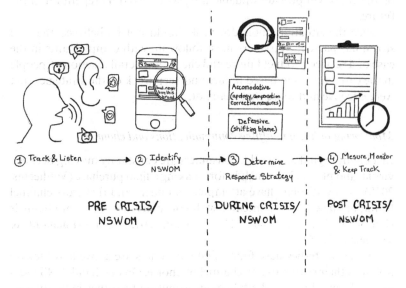

*Figure 5.1* Dealing with NSWOM and brand crisis
Courtesy of Nayla Idriss

## Notes

1  An ounce of prevention is better than a pound of cure
2  On June 2nd 2020, millions of people and brands posted a plain black square on their social media accounts for #blackouttuesday in solidarity with the Black Lives Matter movement following the killing of George Floyd.
3  Visual representation of facial expressions using characters, typically used in online messages.

# Conclusion

*You have a very important business meeting in New York tonight. You had a busy schedule at work so you were forced to take a flight on the same day. As it turns out, the flight got delayed. You try to reach out to the airline employees but no one is giving you an answer. You wait a bit longer but now the flight's cancelled. You're pissed off. It's too late to book another flight, you're not going to make your meeting. You ask to speak to a manager, they give you a number to voice your complaint. You call for days, but you don't get any answer on how to get your money back. What do you do? Forget about it or resort to social media?*

If you still think the second option is a SNS user's first option, then I might need to write another book!

Social media has empowered the consumer to take charge of their consumptions. In the age of a rise of ethical and more conscious consumption they are demanding authenticity and consciousness in their consumption choices. They are also requiring more transparency; dishonest marketing stunts are not effective anymore. It's not enough to say you support diversity or the medical staff working hard during the pandemic. You have to prove it, show the steps you've taken to achieve actual support, monetary or not. Somehow brands that claim to support cause but are later exposed as doing the exact opposite of the essence of those causes are more reprimanded than brands who do not show support to the cause at all. Honesty is essential in the brand–consumer relationship, today, it's so easy to verify it. Many groups and profiles on social network sites have been created to hold companies accountable. They denounce unethical conduct as well as product and service failures and encourage their followers to share their stories, giving NSWOM a whole new platform and an even wider reach.

Consumers resort to NSWOM for a variety of reasons including managing their perceived image, regulating their negative emotions and seeking damage repair. Beyond their individualistic needs they are also motivated by altruistic reasons, such as bonding with their peers, warning and informing them about the pitfalls of products/services.

When SNS users scroll through their feeds, the more a message is vivid and emotionally charged, the more likely they will process the information and potentially share it.

Therefore, brands can't make value-based failures just as much as they can't afford to make product/service-related failures. The slightest failure can quickly escalate into a firestorm if not handled promptly and correctly. Even if it's close to impossible to avoid making any mishap, it is possible to limit the consequences of potential crises. Evidently, there is no easy fix or a magic marker that will wipe away NSWOM or a one size fits all solution. What is certain is that brands must encourage dialogue with their fans and potential consumers. Each brand might carefully analyze its actions and consumers' reactions to establish future do's and don'ts.

Careful consideration should be given to the tone used in responses and the content of the response. An empathetic human voice is preferred. People will remember a brand response more than the reasons of the failure. So why not make it memorable? Delighting them. A possible way to achieve it is by getting creative. Why not give consumers the chance to adjust amendments to a failure? Co-creation can help improve a brand's online reputation (Miled et al., 2018), resorting to this exchange in the midst of a crisis can really show care and possibly turn a dissatisfaction into a delightful experience.

If the brand responses succeeded in delighting customers, especially in the case of a product failure, it might be relevant to encourage now-delighted-complainants to spread the word among their network, the *positive* word.

# References

Aaron Allen & Associates. 2018. *How Domino's Turnaround Gained Nearly $12B In Enterprise Value*. [online] Available at: <https://aaronallen.com/blog/dominos-turnaround> [Accessed 29 April 2020].

Aghakhani, N., Kalantar, H., and Salehan, M. 2016. Adoption of implicit eWOM in Facebook: an affect-as-information theory perspective twenty-second Americas conference on information systems, San Diego.

Albert, R., Jeong, H. and Barabási, A.L., 1999. Internet: diameter of the world-wide web. *Nature*, 401(6749), p.130.

Allport, G.W. and Postman, L. 1946. An analysis of rumor. *Public Opinion Quarterly*, 10(4), pp.501–517.

Allsop, D.T., Bassett, B.R. and Hoskins, J.A. 2007. Word-of-mouth research: principles and applications. *Journal of Advertising Research*, 47(4), pp.398–411.

Amblee, N. and Bui, T. 2008. Can brand reputation improve the odds of being reviewed on-line? *International Journal of Electronic Commerce*, 12(3), pp.11–28.

Anderson, E.W. 1998. Customer satisfaction and word of mouth. *Journal of Service Research*, 1(1), pp.5–17.

Ardelet, C. and Brial, B. 2011. Influence of the recommendations of Internet users: the role of social presence and expertise. *Recherche et Applications en Marketing (English Edition)*, 26(3), pp.45–67.

Argyriou, E. and Melewar, T.C. 2011. Consumer attitudes revisited: a review of attitude theory in marketing research. *International Journal of Management Reviews*, 13(4), pp.431–451.

Arndt, J., 1967. Role of product-related conversations in the diffusion of a new product. *Journal of Marketing Research*, 4(3), pp.291–295.

Aune, R.K. and Kikuchi, T. 1993. Effects of language intensity similarity on perceptions of credibility relational attributions, and persuasion. *Journal of Language and Social Psychology*, 12(3), pp.224–238.

Awad, N.F. and Ragowsky, A. 2008. Establishing trust in electronic commerce through online word of mouth: an examination across genders. *Journal of Management Information Systems*, 24(4), pp.101–121.

Axsom, D., Yates, S. and Chaiken, S. 1987. Audience response as a heuristic cue in persuasion. *Journal of Personality and Social Psychology*, 53(1), p.30.

Bagozzi, R.P. 1983. A holistic methodology for modeling consumer response to innovation. *Operations Research*, 31(1), pp.128–176.

Bagozzi, R.P., Gopinath, M. and Nyer, P.U. 1999. The role of emotions in marketing. *Journal of the Academy of Marketing Science*, 27(2), p.184.

Bailey, A.A. 2005. Consumer awareness and use of product review websites. *Journal of Interactive Advertising*, 6(1), pp.68–81.

Balaji, M.S. and Sarkar, A. 2013. Does successful recovery mitigate failure severity? *International Journal of Emerging Markets*, 8(1), pp. 65–81.

Balaji, M.S., Khong, K.W. and Chong, A.Y.L. 2016. Determinants of negative word-of-mouth communication using social networking sites. *Information & Management*, 53(4), pp.528–540.

Bammel, G. and Burrus-Bammel, L.L. 1996. Leisure and human behavior. *Journal of Leisure Research*, 28(2), p.135.

Bansal, H.S. and Voyer, P.A. 2000. Word-of-mouth processes within a services purchase decision context. *Journal of Service Research*, 3(2), pp.166–177.

Barabási, A.L. 2002. *Linked: The new science of networks*. Cambridge, MA: Perseus Publishing.

Barclay, L.J. and Skarlicki, D.P. 2009. Healing the wounds of organizational injustice: examining the benefits of expressive writing. *Journal of Applied Psychology*, 94(2), p.511.

Barkin, S.L., Finch, S.A., Ip, E.H., Scheindlin, B., Craig, J.A., Steffes, J., Weiley, V., Slora, E., Altman, D. and Wasserman, R.C. 2008. Is office-based counseling about media use, timeouts, and firearm storage effective? Results from a cluster-randomized, controlled trial. *Pediatrics*, 122(1), p.e15.

Bechwati, N.N. and Morrin, M. 2003. Outraged consumers: getting even at the expense of getting a good deal. *Journal of Consumer Psychology*, 13(4), pp.440–453.

Belk, R.W. 1988. Possessions and the extended self. *Journal of Consumer Research*, 15(2), pp.139–168.

Benoit, W.L. 1997. Image repair discourse and crisis communication. *Public Relations Review*, 23(2), pp.177–186.

Berger, J. and Iyengar, R. 2013. Communication channels and word of mouth: how the medium shapes the message. *Journal of Consumer Research*, 40(3), pp.567–579.

Berger, J. and Milkman, K.L. 2012. What makes online content viral?. *Journal of Marketing Research*, 49(2), pp.192–205.

Berger, J. 2014. Word of mouth and interpersonal communication: a review and directions for future research. *Journal of Consumer Psychology*, 24(4), pp. 586–607.

Bhandari, M. and Rodgers, S. 2018. What does the brand say? Effects of brand feedback to negative eWOM on brand trust and purchase intentions. *International Journal of Advertising*, 37(1), pp.125–141.

Bhattacherjee, A. and Sanford, C. 2006. Influence processes for information technology acceptance: an elaboration likelihood model. *MIS Quarterly*, pp.805–825.

Bickart, B. and Schindler, R.M. 2001. Internet forums as influential sources of consumer information. *Journal of Interactive Marketing*, 15(3), pp.31–40.

Bone, P.F. 1992. Determinants of word-of-mouth communications during product consumption. *ACR North American Advances*.

Bone, P.F. 1995. Word-of-mouth effects on short-term and long-term product judgments. *Journal of Business Research*, 32(3), pp.213–223.

Borah, A. and Tellis, G.J. 2016. Halo (spillover) effects in social media: do product recalls of one brand hurt or help rival brands?. *Journal of Marketing Research*, 53(2), pp.143–160.

Bowers, J.W. 1963. Language intensity, social introversion, and attitude change. *Speech Monographs*, 30(4), pp. 345–352.

Boyd, D.M. and Ellison, N.B. 2007. Social network sites: definition, history, and scholarship. *Journal of Computer-mediated Communication*, 13(1), pp.210–230.

Breazeale, M. 2009. Word of Mouse: an assessment of electronic word-of-mouth research. *International Journal of Market Research*, 51(3), pp.1–19.

Breck, E. and Cardie, C. 2004. Playing the telephone game: determining the hierarchical structure of perspective and speech expressions. In *Proceedings of the 20th international conference on Computational Linguistics* (p. 120). Association for Computational Linguistics.

Breitsohl, J. and Garrod, B. 2016. Assessing tourists' cognitive, emotional and behavioural reactions to an unethical destination incident. *Tourism Management*, 54, pp.209–220.

Bromwich, J. 2016. *Six degrees f separation? Facebook finds a smaller number*. [online] Nytimes.com. Available at: <www.nytimes.com/2016/02/05/technology/six-degrees-of-separation-facebook-finds-a-smaller-number.html> [Accessed 3 April 2020].

Brown, J. J., & Reingen, P. H. 1987. Social ties and word-of-mouth referral behavior. *Journal of Consumer Research*, 14(3), pp.350–362.

Butler, E.A., Egloff, B., Wlhelm, F.H., Smith, N.C., Erickson, E.A. and Gross, J.J. 2003. The social consequences of expressive suppression. *Emotion*, 3(1), p.48.

Buttle, F.A. 1998. Word of mouth: understanding and managing referral marketing. *Journal of Strategic Marketing*, 6(3), pp.241–254.

Cameron, D. 2009. Attitude is everything: final report. *Report of Research Findings to World Education Development Group*.

Chaiken, S. and Eagly, A.H. 1976. Communication modality as a determinant of message persuasiveness and message comprehensibility. *Journal of Personality and Social Psychology*, 34(4), p.605.

Chaiken, S. and Eagly, A.H. 1983. Communication modality as a determinant of persuasion: The role of communicator salience. *Journal of Personality and Social Psychology*, 45(2), p.241.

Chaiken, S. 1980. Heuristic versus systematic information processing and the use of source versus message cues in persuasion. *Journal of Personality and Social Psychology*, 39(5), p.752.

Chakravarty, A., Liu, Y. and Mazumdar, T. 2010. The differential effects of online word-of-mouth and critics' reviews on pre-release movie evaluation. *Journal of Interactive Marketing*, 24(3), pp.185–197.

Chang, H.H. and Wu, L.H. 2014. An examination of negative e-WOM adoption: brand commitment as a moderator. *Decision Support Systems*, 59, pp.206–218.

Chang, H.H. and Wu, L.H. 2014. An examination of negative e-WOM adoption: brand commitment as a moderator. *Decision Support Systems*, 59, pp.206–218.

Cheung, C.M. and Thadani, D.R. 2012. The impact of electronic word-of-mouth communication: a literature analysis and integrative model. *Decision Support Systems*, 54(1), pp.461–470.

Cheung, C.M., Lee, M.K. and Rabjohn, N. 2008. The impact of electronic word-of-mouth: the adoption of online opinions in online customer communities. *Internet Research*, 18(3), pp.229–247.

Cheung, C.M., Lee, M.K. and Thadani, D.R. 2009. September. The impact of positive electronic word-of-mouth on consumer online purchasing decision. In *World Summit on Knowledge Society* (pp. 501–510).

Cheung, C.M.Y., Sia, C.L. and Kuan, K.K. 2012. Is this review believable? A study of factors affecting the credibility of online consumer reviews from an ELM perspective. *Journal of the Association for Information Systems*, 13(8), p.618.

Cheung, M.Y., Luo, C., Sia, C.L. and Chen, H. 2009. Credibility of electronic word-of-mouth: Iinformational and normative determinants of on-line consumer recommendations. *International Journal of Electronic Commerce*, 13(4), pp.9–38.

Chevalier, J.A. and Mayzlin, D. 2006. The effect of word of mouth on sales: online book reviews. *Journal of Marketing Research*, 43(3), pp.345–354.

Chu, K.M. (2009). A study of members' helping behaviors in online community. *Internet Research*, 19(3), 279–292.

Chu, S.C. and Kim, Y. 2011. Determinants of consumer engagement in electronic word-of-mouth (eWOM) in social networking sites. *International Journal of Advertising*, 30(1), pp.47–75.

Chung, C.M. and Darke, P.R. 2006. The consumer as advocate: self-relevance, culture, and word-of-mouth. *Marketing Letters*, 17(4), pp.269–279.

Clow, K.E., James, K.E. and Stanley, S. 2008. Does source credibility affect how credit cards are marketed to college students. *The Marketing Management Journal*, 18(2), pp.168–178.

Cohen, J.B. and Areni, C.S. 1991. Affect and consumer behavior. 188.

Constine, J. 2017. Snapchat hits a disappointing 166M daily users, growing only slightly faster. *Tech Crunch Website*.

Coombs, W.T. and Holladay, S.J. 2007. The negative communication dynamic. *Journal of Communication Management*. 11(4), pp. 300–312.

Copulsky, J.R. 2011. *Brand Resilience: Managing Risk and Recovery in a High-Speed World*. St. Martin's Press.

Court, D., Elzinga, D., Mulder, S. and Vetvik, O.J. 2009. The consumer decision journey. *McKinsey Quarterly*, 3(3), pp.96–107.

Datoo, S. 2020. *Zuckerberg Loses $7 Billion As Firms Boycott Facebook Ads*. [online] Bloomberg.com. Available at: <www.bloomberg.com/news/articles/2020-06-27/mark-zuckerberg-loses-7-billion-as-companies-drop-facebook-ads> [Accessed 2 July 2020].

Davidson III, W.N., Worrell, D.L. and El-Jelly, A. 1995. Influencing managers to change unpopular corporate behavior through boycotts and divestitures: a stock market test. *Business & Society*, 34(2), pp.171–196.

Davis, A. and Khazanchi, D. 2008. An empirical study of online word of mouth as a predictor for multi-product category e-commerce sales. *Electronic Markets*, 18(2), pp.130–141.

De Angelis, M., Bonezzi, A., Peluso, A.M., Rucker, D.D. and Costabile, M. 2012. On braggarts and gossips: a self-enhancement account of word-of-mouth generation and transmission. *Journal of Marketing Research*, 49(4), pp.551–563.

De Bruyn, A. and Lilien, G.L. 2008. A multi-stage model of word-of-mouth influence through viral marketing. *International Journal of Research in Marketing*, 25(3), pp.151–163.

De Matos, C.A. and Rossi, C.A.V. 2008. Word-of-mouth communications in marketing: a meta-analytic review of the antecedents and moderators. *Journal of the Academy of Marketing Science*, 36(4), pp.578–596.

DeBono, K.G. and Telesca, C. 1990. The influence of source physical attractiveness on advertising effectiveness: a functional perspective 1. *Journal of Applied Social Psychology*, 20(17), pp.1383–1395.

Dellarocas, C. and Narayan, R. 2007. Tall heads vs. long tails: Do consumer reviews increase the informational inequality between hit and niche products? *Robert H. Smith School of Business Research Paper*, (06-056).

Dellarocas, C., Zhang, X. and Awad, N.F. 2007. Exploring the value of online product reviews in forecasting sales: the case of motion pictures. *Journal of Interactive Marketing*, 21(4), pp.23–45.

Dens, N., De Pelsmacker, P. and Purnawirawan, N. 2015. We (b) care. *Journal of Service Management*, 26(3), pp. 486–515.

Derbaix, C. and Vanhamme, J. 2003. Inducing word-of-mouth by eliciting surprise–a pilot investigation. *Journal of Economic Psychology*, 24(1), pp.99–116.

Deutsch, M. and Gerard, H.B. 1955. A study of normative and informational social influences upon individual judgment. *The Journal of Abnormal and Social Psychology*, 51(3), p.629.

Dichter, E. 1966. How word-of-mouth advertising works. *Harvard Business Review*, 44(6), pp.147–160.

Doerr, B., Fouz, M. and Friedrich, T. 2012. Why rumors spread fast in social networks. *Communications of the ACM*, 55(6), pp.70–75.

Doh, S.J. and Hwang, J.S. 2009. How consumers evaluate eWOM (electronic word-of-mouth) messages. *CyberPsychology & Behavior*, 12(2), pp.193–197.

Dwyer, C. 2007, January. Digital relationships in the "myspace" generation: results from a qualitative study. In *2007 40th Annual Hawaii International Conference on System Sciences (HICSS'07)* (p. 19). IEEE.

Eagly, A.H., Wood, W. and Chaiken, S. 1978. Causal inferences about communicators and their effect on opinion change. *Journal of Personality and Social Psychology*, 36(4), p.424.

East, R. and Uncles, M.D. 2008. In praise of retrospective surveys. *Journal of Marketing Management*, 24(9–10), pp.929–944.

East, R., Hammond, K. and Lomax, W. 2008. Measuring the impact of positive and negative word of mouth on brand purchase probability. *International Journal of Research in Marketing*, 25(3), pp.215–224.

Edelman, D.C. 2010. Branding in the digital age. *Harvard Business Review*, 88(12), pp.62–69.

Ekman, P. 1992. An argument for basic emotions. *Cognition & Emotion*, 6(3–4), pp.169–200.

Ellison, N.B. 2007. Social network sites: definition, history, and scholarship. *Journal of Computer-mediated Communication*, 13(1), pp.210–230.

Ellison, N.B., Steinfield, C. and Lampe, C. 2007. The benefits of Facebook "friends:" social capital and college students' use of online social network sites. *Journal of Computer-mediated Communication*, 12(4), pp.1143–1168.

Engel, J.F., Blackwell, R.D., and Miniard, P.W. (1993). *Consumer Behavior* (8th ed.). Fort Worth: Dryden Press.

Eysenbach, G., 2008. *Credibility of Health Information and Digital Media: New Perspectives and Implications for Youth* (pp. 123–154). MacArthur Foundation Digital Media and Learning Initiative.

Farah, M.F. and Newman, A.J. 2010. Exploring consumer boycott intelligence using a socio-cognitive approach. *Journal of Business Research*, 63(4), pp.347–355.

Feldman, R. 2013. Techniques and applications for sentiment analysis. *Communications of the ACM*, 56(4), pp.82–89.

Festinger, L. (1964). *Conflict, Decision, and Dissonance*. Stanford, CA: Stanford University Press.

Festinger, L. 1957. *A Theory of Cognitive Dissonance*. Evanston, IL: Row, Peterson.

Fitzsimons, G.J. and Lehmann, D.R. 2004. Reactance to recommendations: when unsolicited advice yields contrary responses. *Marketing Science*, 23(1), pp.82–94.

Flanagin, A.J. and Metzger, M.J. 2007. The role of site features, user attributes, and information verification behaviors on the perceived credibility of web-based information. *New Media & Society*, 9(2), pp.319–342.

Folse, J.A.G., Porter III, M., Godbole, M.B. and Reynolds, K.E. 2016. The effects of negatively valenced emotional expressions in online reviews on the reviewer, the review, and the product. *Psychology & Marketing*, 33(9), pp.747–760.

Forgas, J. P. 1995. Mood and judgment: the affect infusion model (AIM). *Psychological Bulletin*, 117(1), 39.

Forman, C., Ghose, A. and Wiesenfeld, B. 2008. Examining the relationship between reviews and sales: the role of reviewer identity disclosure in electronic markets. *Information Systems Research*, 19(3), pp.291–313.

Friedman, M. 1985. Consumer boycotts in the United States, 1970–1980: contemporary events in historical perspective. *Journal of Consumer Affairs*, 19(1), pp.96–117.

Friedman, M., 1999. *Consumer Boycotts: Effecting Change Through the Marketplace and the Media*. Psychology Press.

Froissart, P. 2008. Rumor. *The International Encyclopedia of Communication*.

Gerard, H.B., and White, G.L. (1983). Post-decisional reevaluation of choice alternatives. *Personality and Social Psychology Bulletin*, 9, pp.365–369.

Gershoff, A.D., Mukherjee, A. and Mukhopadhyay, A. 2003. Consumer acceptance of online agent advice: extremity and positivity effects. *Journal of Consumer Psychology*, 13(1–2), pp.161–170.

Ghosh, T. 2017. Managing negative reviews: the persuasive role of webcare characteristics. *Journal of Internet Commerce*, 16(2), pp.148–173.

Godes, D. and Mayzlin, D. 2004. Firm-created word-of-mouth communication: A field-based quasi-experiment. *HBS Marketing Research Paper* (04-03).

Godes, D. and Mayzlin, D. 2004. Using online conversations to study word-of-mouth communication. *Marketing Science*, 23(4), pp.545–560.

Goldsmith, R.E. and Horowitz, D. 2006. Measuring motivations for online opinion seeking. *Journal of Interactive Advertising*, 6(2), pp.2–14.

Goyette, I., Ricard, L., Bergeron, J. and Marticotte, F. 2010. e-WOM Scale: word-of-mouth measurement scale for e-services context. *Canadian Journal of Administrative Sciences/Revue Canadienne des Sciences de l'Administration*, 27(1), pp.5–23.

Granovetter, M. 1982. Alienation reconsidered: The strength of weak ties. *Connections*, 5(2): 4–15.

Grappi, S., Romani, S. and Bagozzi, R.P. 2013. Consumer response to corporate irresponsible behavior: moral emotions and virtues. *Journal of Business Research*, 66(10), pp.1814–1821.

Greenwald, A.G. and Leavitt, C. 1984. Audience involvement in advertising: four levels. *Journal of Consumer Research*, 11(1), pp.581–592.

Greenwald, A.G. 1968. Cognitive learning, cognitive response to persuasion, and attitude change. *Psychological Foundations of Attitudes*, 1968, pp.147–170.

Gross, J.J. 2008. Emotion regulation. *Handbook of Emotions*, 3(3), pp.497–513.

Gruen, T.W., Osmonbekov, T. and Czaplewski, A.J. 2006. eWOM: the impact of customer-to-customer online know-how exchange on customer value and loyalty. *Journal of Business Research*, 59(4), pp.449–456.

Guichard, N. and Vanheems, R. 2004. *Comportement du consommateur et de l'acheteur*. Editions Bréal.

Hamilton, M.A. 1998. Message variables that mediate and moderate the effect of equivocal language on source credibility. *Journal of Language and Social Psychology*, 17(1), pp.109–143.

Hamouda, M. and Srarfi Tabbane, R. 2014. Impact du BAO électronique sur l'intention d'achat du consommateur: le rôle modérateur de l'âge et du genre. *La Revue Gestion et Organisation*, 6(1), pp.39–46.

Hanna, N. and Wozniak, R. 2001. *Consumer behavior: An applied approach* (Doctoral dissertation, Univerza v Mariboru, Ekonomsko-poslovna fakulteta).

Harrison-Walker, L.J. 2001. The measurement of word-of-mouth communication and an investigation of service quality and customer commitment as potential antecedents. *Journal of Service Research*, 4(1), pp.60–75.

Hawkins, S.A. and Hoch, S.J. 1992. Low-involvement learning: memory without evaluation. *Journal of Consumer Research*, 19(2), pp.212–225.

Henderson, S. and Gilding, M. 2004. 'I've never clicked this much with anyone in my life': trust and hyperpersonal communication in online friendships. *New Media & Society*, 6(4), pp.487–506.

Hennig-Thurau, T., Gwinner, K.P., Walsh, G. and Gremler, D.D. 2004. Electronic word-of-mouth via consumer-opinion platforms: what motivates consumers to articulate themselves on the internet? *Journal of Interactive Marketing*, 18(1), pp.38–52.

Hennig-Thurau, T., Malthouse, E.C., Friege, C., Gensler, S., Lobschat, L., Rangaswamy, A. and Skiera, B. 2010. The impact of new media on customer relationships. *Journal of Service Research*, 13(3), pp.311–330.

Herr, P.M., Kardes, F.R. and Kim, J. 1991. Effects of word-of-mouth and product-attribute information on persuasion: an accessibility-diagnosticity perspective. *Journal of Consumer Research*, 17(4), pp.454–462.

Hervé, L. 2019. Les 50 chiffres à connaître sur les médias sociaux en 2019. *BDM*. Available at: www.blogdumoderateur.com/50-chiffres-medias-sociaux-2019/ [Accessed March 23, 2019].

Hirschman, E.C. and Holbrook, M.B. 1982. Hedonic consumption: emerging concepts, methods and propositions. *The Journal of Marketing*, 46(3), pp.92–101.

Hoffmann, S. 2011. Anti-consumption as a means to save jobs. European Journal of Marketing, 45(11/12), pp. 1702–1714.

Hogg, M.K. 1998. Anti-constellations: exploring the impact of negation on consumption. *Journal of Marketing Management*, 14(1–3), pp.133–158.

Holbrook, M.B. and Hirschman, E.C. 1982. The experiential aspects of consumption: consumer fantasies, feelings, and fun. *Journal of Consumer Research*, 9(2), pp.132–140.

Holloway, B.B. & Beatty, S.E. 2003. Service failure in online retailing a recovery opportunity. *Journal of Service Research*, 6(1), 92–105.

Homburg, C., Ehm, L. and Artz, M. 2015. Measuring and managing consumer sentiment in an online community environment. *Journal of Marketing Research*, 52(5), pp.629–641.

Hornik, J., Satchi, R.S., Cesareo, L. and Pastore, A. 2015. Information dissemination via electronic word-of-mouth: good news travels fast, bad news travels faster! *Computers in Human Behavior*, 45, pp.273–280.

Houston, M.J. and Rothschild, M.L. 1977. *A paradigm for research on consumer involvement*. Graduate School of Business, University of Wisconsin-Madison.

Hovland, C.I. and Weiss, W. 1951. The influence of source credibility on communication effectiveness. *Public Opinion Quarterly*, 15(4), pp.635–650.

Hovland, C.I., Janis, I.L. and Kelley, H.H. 1953. Communication and Persuasion; psychological studies of opinion change. New Haven, CN: Yale University Press.

*How Domino's Turnaround Gained Nearly $12B In Enterprise Value*. [online] *Public Relations Review*, 23(2), pp.177–186. [Accessed 29 April 2020].

Hu, N., Liu, L. and Zhang, J.J. 2008. Do online reviews affect product sales? The role of reviewer characteristics and temporal effects. *Information Technology and Management*, 9(3), pp.201–214.

Huang, M., Cai, F., Tsang, A.S. and Zhou, N. 2011. Making your online voice loud: the critical role of WOM information. *European Journal of Marketing*, 45(7/8), pp.1277–1297.

Huang, P., Lurie, N.H. and Mitra, S. 2009. Searching for experience on the web: an empirical examination of consumer behavior for search and experience goods. *Journal of Marketing*, 73(2), pp.55–69.

Hung, K.H. and Li, S.Y. 2007. The influence of eWOM on virtual consumer communities: social capital, consumer learning, and behavioral outcomes. *Journal of Advertising Research*, 47(4), pp.485–495.

Iyer, R. and Muncy, J.A. 2008. Service recovery in marketing education: it's what we do that counts. *Journal of Marketing Education*, 30(1), pp.21–32.

Jarvis, J. 2005. My Dell Hell. *The Guardian*, 29.

Jin, B., Yong Park, J. and Kim, J. 2008.Cross-cultural examination of the relationships among firm reputation, e-satisfaction, e-trust, and e-loyalty. *International Marketing Review*, 25(3), pp.324–337.

Jin, X.L., Cheung, C.M., Lee, M.K. and Chen, H.P. 2009. How to keep members using the information in a computer-supported social network. *Computers in Human Behavior*, 25(5), pp.1172–1181.

Kahr, A., Nyffenegger, B., Krohmer, H. and Hoyer, W.D. 2016. When hostile consumers wreak havoc on your brand: the phenomenon of consumer brand sabotage. *Journal of Marketing*, 80(3), pp.25–41.

Kamins, M.A., Folkes, V.S. and Perner, L. 1997. Consumer responses to rumors: good news, bad news. *Journal of Consumer Psychology*, 6(2), pp.165–187.

Kapferer, J.N., 1990. *Rumors*. New Brunswick, NJ: Transaction Publishers.

Kaplan, A.M. and Haenlein, M. 2010. Users of the world, unite! The challenges and opportunities of social media. *Business Horizons*, 53(1), pp.59–68.

Karakaya, F. and Barnes, N.G. 2010. Impact of online reviews of customer care experience on brand or company selection. *Journal of Consumer Marketing*, 27(5), 447–457.

Karmarkar, U.R. and Tormala, Z.L. 2010. Believe me, I have no idea what I'm talking about: the effects of source certainty on consumer involvement and persuasion. *Journal of Consumer Research*, 36(6), pp.1033–1049.

Kavaliauskė, M. and Simanavičiūtė, E. 2015. Brand avoidance: relations between brand-related stimuli and negative emotions. *Organizations and Markets in Emerging Economies*, 6, pp.44–77.

Keaveney, S.M. 1995. Customer switching behavior in service industries: an exploratory study. *Journal of Marketing*, 59(2), pp.71–82.

Kim, P.H., Dirks, K.T., Cooper, C.D. and Ferrin, D.L. 2006. When more blame is better than less: the implications of internal vs. external attributions for the repair of trust after a competence-vs. integrity-based trust violation. *Organizational Behavior and Human Decision Processes*, 99(1), pp.49–65.

Kim, W. and Rifon, N.J. 2016. Understanding the impact of negative electronic word-of-mouth on consumer: the role of emotional intensity and tie-strength. In *American Academy of Advertising. Conference. Proceedings (Online)* (p. 128). American Academy of Advertising.

King, R.A., Racherla, P. and Bush, V.D. 2014. What we know and don't know about online word-of-mouth: a review and synthesis of the literature. *Journal of Interactive Marketing*, 28(3), pp.167–183.

Klein, J.G., Smith, N.C. and John, A. 2002. Why we boycott: consumer motivations for boycott participation and marketer responses. London Business School (June), pp.1–41.

Klein, J.G., Smith, N.C. and John, A. 2004. Why we boycott: consumer motivations for boycott participation. *Journal of Marketing*, 68(3), pp.92–109.

Kozinets, R.V., De Valck, K., Wojnicki, A.C. and Wilner, S.J. 2010. Networked narratives: understanding word-of-mouth marketing in online communities. *Journal of Marketing*, 74(2), pp.71–89.

Krosnick, J.A., Boninger, D.S., Chuang, Y.C., Berent, M.K. and Carnot, C.G. 1993. Attitude strength: one construct or many related constructs? *Journal of Personality and Social Psychology*, 65(6), p.1132.

Ladhari, R. 2007. The effect of consumption emotions on satisfaction and word-of-mouth communications. *Psychology & Marketing*, 24(12), pp.1085–1108.

Lai, M.K. and Aritejo, B.A. 2010, June. Anti-consumption and consumer resistance: a conceptual review. CAR/NACRE Symposium, Marseilles, France.

Lampe, C., Ellison, N. and Steinfield, C. 2006, November. A Face (book) in the crowd: ocial searching vs. social browsing. In Proceedings of the 2006 20th anniversary conference on Computer supported cooperative work (pp. 167–170). ACM.

Lasswell, H. D. 1948. The structure and function of communication in society. In L. Bryson (Ed.), *Communication of Ideas* (pp. 37–51). New York: Harper and Row.

Latiff, Z.A. and Safiee, N.A.S. 2015. New business set up for branding strategies on social media–Instagram. *Procedia Computer Science*, 72, pp.13–23.

Lau, G.T. and Ng, S. 2001. Individual and situational factors influencing negative word-of-mouth behaviour. *Canadian Journal of Administrative Sciences/ Revue Canadienne des Sciences de l'Administration*, 18(3), pp.163–178.

Lee, B.K. (2005). Hong Kong consumers' evaluation in an airline crash: a path model analysis. *Journal of Public Relations Research*, 17(4), 363–391.

Lee, C.H. and Cranage, D.A. 2014. Toward understanding consumer processing of negative online word-of-mouth communication: the roles of opinion consensus and organizational response strategies. *Journal of Hospitality & Tourism Research*, 38(3), pp.330–360.

Lee, H., Park, T., Moon, H.K., Yang, Y. and Kim, C. 2009. Corporate philanthropy, attitude towards corporations, and purchase intentions: a South Korea study. *Journal of Business Research*, 62(10), pp.939–946.

Lee, J., Park, D.H. and Han, I. 2011. The different effects of online consumer reviews on consumers' purchase intentions depending on trust in online shopping malls. *Internet Research*, 21(2), 187–206.

Lee, K.T. and Koo, D.M. 2012. Effects of attribute and valence of e-WOM on message adoption: moderating roles of subjective knowledge and regulatory focus. *Computers in Human Behavior*, 28(5), pp.1974–1984.

Lee, M. and Youn, S. 2009. Electronic word of mouth (eWOM) How eWOM platforms influence consumer product judgement. *International Journal of Advertising*, 28(3), pp.473–499.

Lee, Y.L. and Song, S. 2010. An empirical investigation of electronic word-of-mouth: Informational motive and corporate response strategy. *Computers in Human Behavior*, 26(5), pp.1073–1080.

Lee, Z.W., Cheung, C.M. and Thadani, D.R. 2012, January. An investigation into the problematic use of Facebook. In *2012 45th Hawaii International Conference on System Sciences* (pp. 1768–1776). IEEE.

Len-Ríos, M.E. and Benoit, W.L. 2004. Gary Condit's image repair strategies: Determined denial and differentiation. *Public Relations Review*, 30(1), pp.95–106.

Litvin, S.W., Goldsmith, R.E. and Pan, B. 2008. Electronic word-of-mouth in hospitality and tourism management. *Tourism Management*, 29(3), pp.458–468.

Labrecque, L.I., vor dem Esche, J., Mathwick, C., Novak, T.P., & Hofacker, C.F. (2013). Consumer power: evolution in the digital age. *Journal of Interactive Marketing*, 27(4), 257–269.

Lyon, L. and Cameron, G.T. 2004. A relational approach examining the interplay of prior reputation and immediate response to a crisis. *Journal of Public Relations Research*, 16(3), pp.213–241.

Mazzarol, T., Sweeney, J.C. and Soutar, G.N. 2007.Conceptualizing word-of-mouth activity, triggers and conditions: an exploratory study. *European Journal of Marketing*, 41(11/12), pp.1475–1494.

Meiners, N.H., Schwarting, U. and Seeberger, B. 2010. The renaissance of word-of-mouth marketing: a 'new' standard in twenty-first century marketing management. *International Journal of Economic Sciences and Applied Research*, 3(2), p.79.

Metzger, M.J. and Flanagin, A.J. 2013. Credibility and trust of information in online environments: The use of cognitive heuristics. *Journal of Pragmatics*, 59, pp.210–220.

Miled, H.C.B., Cros, S., Pratlong, F., Bonev, B. and Poirier, R. 2018. Réseaux sociaux et e-réputation: le cas de la SCNF. *Vie sciences de l'entreprise*, (2), pp.103–122.

Mills, J. and Jellison, J.M. 1967. Effect on opinion change of how desirable the communication is to the audience the communicator addressed. *Journal of Personality and Social Psychology*, 6(1), p.98.

Mitchell, A.A. 1981. The dimensions of advertising involvement. *ACR North American Advances*, 8, pp. 25–30.

Munzel, A. 2015. Malicious practice of fake reviews: experimental insight into the potential of contextual indicators in assisting consumers to detect deceptive opinion spam. *Recherche et Applications en Marketing (English Edition)*, 30(4), pp.24–50.

Naylor, R.W., Lamberton, C.P. and West, P.M. 2012. Beyond the "like" button: the impact of mere virtual presence on brand evaluations and purchase intentions in social media settings. *Journal of Marketing*, 76(6), pp.105–120.

Ng, S., David, M.E. and Dagger, T.S. 2011. Generating positive word-of-mouth in the service experience. *Managing Service Quality: An International Journal*, 21(2), pp.133–151.

Nyer, P.U. and Gopinath, M. 2005. Effects of complaining versus negative word of mouth on subsequent changes in satisfaction: the role of public commitment. *Psychology & Marketing*, 22(12), pp.937–953.

Olshavsky, R.W. and Granbois, D.H. 1979. Consumer decision making—fact or fiction? *Journal of Consumer Research*, 6(2), pp.93–100.

Ott, L. and Theunissen, P. 2015. Reputations at risk: engagement during social media crises. *Public Relations Review*, 41(1), pp.97–102.

Packard, G. and Wooten, D.B. 2013. Compensatory knowledge signaling in consumer word-of-mouth. *Journal of Consumer Psychology*, 23(4), pp.434–450.

Pan, L.Y. and Chiou, J.S. 2011. How much can you trust online information? Cues for perceived trustworthiness of consumer-generated online information. *Journal of Interactive Marketing*, 25(2), pp.67–74.

Park, C. and Lee, T.M. 2009. Information direction, website reputation and eWOM effect: a moderating role of product type. *Journal of Business Research*, 62(1), pp.61–67.

Park, D.H. and Kim, S. 2008.The effects of consumer knowledge on message processing of electronic word-of-mouth via online consumer reviews. *Electronic Commerce Research and Applications*, 7(4), pp.399–410.

Park, D.H., Lee, J. and Han, I. 2007. The effect of on-line consumer reviews on consumer purchasing intention: the moderating role of involvement. *International Journal of Electronic Commerce*, 11(4), pp.125–148.

Petty, R.E. and Cacioppo, J.T. 1986. The elaboration likelihood model of persuasion. In *Communication and Persuasion* (pp. 1–24). New York, NY: Springer.

Petty, R.E., Cacioppo, J.T. and Goldman, R. 1981. Personal involvement as a determinant of argument-based persuasion. *Journal of Personality and Social Psychology*, 41(5), p.847.

Petty, R.E., Cacioppo, J.T. and Schumann, D. 1983. Central and peripheral routes to advertising effectiveness: the moderating role of involvement. *Journal of Consumer Research*, 10(2), pp.135–146.

Petty, R.E. and J.T. Cacioppo, 1986. The elaboration likelihood model of persuasion, In *Advances in Experimental Social Psychology*, L. Berkwotz, editor. Academic Press Inc., pp.123–205.

Price, L.L. and Feick, L.F. 1984. The role of interpersonal sources in external search: An informational perspective. *ACR North American Advances*, 11, pp. 250–255.

Pruitt, S.W. and Friedman, M. 1986. Determining the effectiveness of consumer boycotts: a stock price analysis of their impact on corporate targets. *Journal of Consumer Policy*, 9(4), pp.375–387.

Qiu, L., Pang, J. and Lim, K.H. 2012. Effects of conflicting aggregated rating on eWOM review credibility and diagnosticity: the moderating role of review valence. *Decision Support Systems*, 54(1), pp.631–643.

ReviewTrackers. 2018. *2018 Reviewtrackers Online Reviews Stats and Survey | Reviewtrackers*. [online] Available at: <www.reviewtrackers.com/reports/online-reviews-survey/> [Accessed 2 March 2020].

Richins, M.L. 1994. Valuing things: the public and private meanings of possessions. *Journal of Consumer Research*, 21(3), pp.504–521.

Riegner, C. 2007. Word of mouth on the web: the impact of Web 2.0 on consumer purchase decisions. *Journal of Advertising Research*, 47(4), pp.436–447.

Rimé, B. 2007. Interpersonal emotion regulation. *Handbook of Emotion Regulation*, 1, pp.466–468.

Ruths, D. and Pfeffer, J. 2014. Social media for large studies of behavior. *Science*, 346(6213), pp.1063–1064.

Schank, R. and Abelson, R.P. 1995. *Knowledge and memory: The real story, Advances in Social Cognition*, Volume VIII. In *Lawrence Erlbaum Associates*.

Sen, S., Gürhan-Canli, Z. and Morwitz, V. 2001. Withholding consumption: a social dilemma perspective on consumer boycotts. *Journal of Consumer Research*, 28(3), pp.399–417.

Sher, P.J. and Lee, S.H. 2009. Consumer skepticism and online reviews: an elaboration likelihood model perspective. *Social Behavior and Personality: An International Journal*, 37(1), pp.137–143.

Shiv, B., Loewenstein, G., Bechara, A., Damasio, H. and Damasio, A.R. 2005. Investment behavior and the negative side of emotion. *Psychological Science*, 16(6), pp.435–439.

Singh, J. 1988. Consumer complaint intentions and behavior: definitional and taxonomical issues. *Journal of Marketing*, 52(1), pp.93–107.

So, K.K.F., King, C., Sparks, B.A. and Wang, Y. 2016. The role of customer engagement in building consumer loyalty to tourism brands. *Journal of Travel Research*, 55(1), pp.64–78.

Söderlund, M., & Rosengren, S. 2007. Receiving word-of-mouth from the service customer: an emotion-based effectiveness assessment. *Journal of Retailing and Consumer Services*, 14(2), 123–136.

## 94    References

Steffes, E.M. and Burgee, L.E. 2009. Social ties and online word of mouth. *Internet Research*, 19(1), pp.42–59.

Stenger, T. and Coutant, A. 2010. Les réseaux sociaux numériques: des discours de promotion à la définition d'un objet et d'une méthodologie de recherche. *HERMES-Journal of Language and Communication in Business*, (44), pp.209–228.

Stieglitz, S. and Dang-Xuan, L. 2013. Emotions and information diffusion in social media—sentiment of microblogs and sharing behavior. *Journal of Management Information Systems*, 29(4), pp.217–248.

Stokes, D., Syed, S.A. and Lomax, W. 2002. Shaping up word of mouth marketing strategy: the case of an independent health club. *Journal of Research in Marketing and Entrepreneurship*, 4(2), pp.119–133.

Storbeck, J. and Clore, G.L. 2008. Affective arousal as information: How affective arousal influences judgments, learning, and memory. *Social and Personality Psychology Compass*, 2(5), pp.1824–1843.

Sun, T., Youn, S., Wu, G. and Kuntaraporn, M. 2006. Online word-of-mouth (or mouse): An exploration of its antecedents and consequences. *Journal of Computer-Mediated Communication*, 11(4), pp.1104–1127.

Sundaram, D.S., Mitra, K., & Webster, C. 1998. Word-of-Mouth communications: a motivational analysis. *Advances in Consumer Research*, 25, 527–53.

Sussman, S.W. and Siegal, W.S. 2003. Informational influence in organizations: an integrated approach to knowledge adoption. *Information Systems Research*, 14(1), pp.47–65.

Sweeney, J.C., Soutar, G.N. and Mazzarol, T. 2012. Word of mouth: measuring the power of individual messages. *European Journal of Marketing*, 46(1/2), pp.237–257.

Sweetin, V.H., Knowles, L.L., Summey, J.H. and McQueen, K.S. 2013. Willingness-to-punish the corporate brand for corporate social irresponsibility. *Journal of Business Research*, 66(10), pp.1822–1830.

*Teens Don't Use Facebook, but They Can't Escape It, Either.* [online] WIRED. Available at: www.wired.com/story/teens-cant-escape-facebook/ [Accessed 23 Jun. 2019], *21*E

Tirunillai, S. and Tellis, G.J. 2012. Does chatter really matter? Dynamics of user-generated content and stock performance. *Marketing Science*, 31(2), pp.198–215.

Towner, T.L. and Dulio, D.A. 2011. An experiment of campaign effects during the YouTube election. *New Media & Society*, 13(4), pp.626–644.

Tulving, E. and Pearlstone, Z. 1966. Availability versus accessibility of information in memory for words. *Journal of Verbal Learning and Verbal Behavior*, 5(4), pp.381–391.

Van Noort, G. and Willemsen, L.M. 2012. Online damage control: the effects of proactive versus reactive webcare interventions in consumer-generated and brand-generated platforms. *Journal of Interactive Marketing*, 26(3), pp.131–140.

Van Noort, G., Willemsen, L.M., Kerkhof, P. and Verhoeven, J.W. 2015. Webcare as an integrative tool for customer care, reputation management, and online marketing: a literature review. In *Integrated Communications in the Postmodern Era* (pp. 77–99). London: Palgrave Macmillan.

Vanheems, R. 2018. *Savoir conseiller et vendre à l'ère post-digitale: Vendeurs et commerciaux: des métiers à réinventer.* Éditions EMS.

Verhagen, T., Nauta, A. and Feldberg, F. 2013. Negative online word-of-mouth: behavioral indicator or emotional release?. *Computers in Human Behavior*, 29(4), pp.1430–1440.

Verplanken, B. 1991. Persuasive communication of risk information: a test of cue versus message processing effects in a field experiment. *Personality and Social Psychology Bulletin*, 17(2), pp.188–193.

Villarroel Ordenes, F., Grewal, D., Ludwig, S., Ruyter, K.D., Mahr, D. and Wetzels, M. 2019. Cutting through content clutter: how speech and image acts drive consumer sharing of social media brand messages. *Journal of Consumer Research*, 45(5), pp.988–1012.

Voorveld, H.A. and van Noort, G. 2014. Social media in advertising campaigns: examining the effects on perceived persuasive intent, campaign and brand responses. *Journal of Creative Communications*, 9(3), pp.253–268.

Wang, L. 2010. The individual's disposition to trust as a moderator of the relationship between electronic words-of-mouth and consumer brand attitude. *Proceedings of the 5th International Conference on Cooperation and Promotion of Information Resources in Science and Technology*, pp. 700–704.

Wasserman, S. and Faust, K. 1994. *Social Network Analysis: Methods and Applications* (Vol. 8). Cambridge University Press.

Wathen, C.N. and Burkell, J. 2002. Believe it or not: factors influencing credibility on the Web. *Journal of the American Society for Information Science and Technology*, 53(2), pp.134–144.

Weitzl, W.J. (2019). Webcare's effect on constructive and vindictive complainants. *Journal of Product & Brand Management.*

Weitzl, W., Hutzinger, C. and Einwiller, S. 2018. An empirical study on how webcare mitigates complainants' failure attributions and negative word-of-mouth. *Computers in Human Behavior*, 89, pp.316–327.

Westbrook, R.A. 1987. Product/consumption-based affective responses and postpurchase processes. *Journal of Marketing Research*, 24(3), pp.258–270.

Willemsen, L., Neijens, P.C. and Bronner, F.A. 2013. Webcare as customer relationship and reputation management? Motives for negative electronic word of mouth and their effect on webcare receptiveness. In *Advances in Advertising Research (Vol. IV)* (pp. 55–69).

Wilson, C., Boe, B., Sala, A., Puttaswamy, K.P. and Zhao, B.Y. 2009, April. User interactions in social networks and their implications. In *Proceedings of the 4th ACM European conference on Computer systems* (pp. 205–218).

Wu, P.C. and Wang, Y.C. 2011. The influences of electronic word-of-mouth message appeal and message source credibility on brand attitude. *Asia Pacific Journal of Marketing and Logistics*, 23(4), pp.448–472.

Xia, L. and Bechwati, N.N. 2008. Word of mouse: the role of cognitive personalization in online consumer reviews. *Journal of Interactive Advertising*, 9(1), pp.3–13.

Xie, K.L., Zhang, Z. and Zhang, Z. 2014. The business value of online consumer reviews and management response to hotel performance. *International Journal of Hospitality Management*, 43, pp.1–12.

Xun, J. and Reynolds, J. 2010. Applying netnography to market research: the case of the online forum. *Journal of Targeting, Measurement and Analysis for Marketing*, 18(1), pp.17–31.

Yayli, A. and Bayram, M. 2012. E-WOM: the effects of online consumer reviews on purchasing decisions. *International Journal of Internet Marketing and Advertising*, 7(1), pp.51–64.

Zadra, J. R., and Clore, G. L. 2011. Emotion and perception: the role of affective information. *Wiley Interdisciplinary Reviews: Cognitive Science*, 2(6), 676–685.

Zeelenberg, M. and Pieters, R. 2004. Beyond valence in customer dissatisfaction: a review and new findings on behavioral responses to regret and disappointment in failed services. *Journal of Business Research*, 57(4), pp.445–455.

# Index

9780367532833